Fossil Fuel Industries
and the Green Economy

Other Books in the Current Controversies Series

Fossil Fuel Industries and the Green Economy

Ariana Agrios, Book Editor

GREENHAVEN PUBLISHING

Published in 2022 by Greenhaven Publishing, LLC
353 3rd Avenue, Suite 255, New York, NY 10010

Articles in Greenhaven Publishing anthologies are often edited for length to meet page
requirements. In addition, original titles of these works are changed to clearly present
the main thesis and to explicitly indicate the author's opinion. Every effort is made to
ensure that Greenhaven Publishing accurately reflects the original intent of the authors.
Every effort has been made to trace the owners of the copyrighted material.

Cover image: Parilov/Shutterstock.com

Library of Congress Cataloging-in-Publication Data

Names: Agrios, Ariana, editor.
Title: Fossil fuel industries and the green economy / Ariana Agrios, book
    editor.
Description: First edition. | New York : Greenhaven Publishing, 2022. |
    Series: Current controversies | Includes bibliographical references and
    index. | Audience: Ages 15+ | Audience: Grades 10-12 | Summary: "Anthology
of diverse perspectives formatted in a point-counterpoint format that debate
use of fossil fuels and the new green economy. Volume introduction and
resource material enhance the viewpoints"— Provided by publisher.
Identifiers: LCCN 2020049375 | ISBN 9781534507869 (library binding) | ISBN
    9781534507845 (paperback) | ISBN 9781534507876 (ebook)
Subjects: LCSH: Fossil fuels—Environmental aspects—Juvenile literature. |
    Renewable energy sources—Juvenile literature.
Classification: LCC TP318.3 .F66 2022 | DDC 662.6—dc23
LC record available at https://lccn.loc.gov/2020049375

Manufactured in the United States of America

Website: http://greenhavenpublishing.com

Chapter 1: Is the Green Economy Financially Superior to the Fossil Fuel Economy?

political, technological, economic, and social problems that require solutions prior to sweeping reform.

Chapter 2: Does the Green Economy Benefit Communities?

Yes: The Green Economy Benefits Communities

Chapter 3: Will Switching to a Green Economy Solve Climate Change?

No: The Green Economy Is Not Financially and Politically Feasible

Foreword

C ontroversy" is a word that has an undeniably unpleasant connotation. It carries a definite negative charge. Controversy can spoil family gatherings, spread a chill around classroom and campus discussion, inflame public discourse, open raw civic wounds, and lead to the ouster of public officials. We often feel that controversy is almost akin to bad manners, a rude and shocking eruption of that which must not be spoken or thought of in polite, tightly guarded society. To avoid controversy, to quell controversy, is often seen as a public good, a victory for etiquette, perhaps even a moral or ethical imperative.

Yet the studious, deliberate avoidance of controversy is also a whitewashing, a denial, a death threat to democracy. It is a false sterilizing and sanitizing and superficial ordering of the messy, ragged, chaotic, at times ugly processes by which a healthy democracy identifies and confronts challenges, engages in passionate debate about appropriate approaches and solutions, and arrives at something like a consensus and a broadly accepted and supported way forward. Controversy is the megaphone, the speaker's corner, the public square through which the citizenry finds and uses its voice. Controversy is the life's blood of our democracy and absolutely essential to the vibrant health of our society.

Our present age is certainly no stranger to controversy. We are consumed by fierce debates about technology, privacy, political correctness, poverty, violence, crime and policing, guns, immigration, civil and human rights, terrorism, militarism, environmental protection, and gender and racial equality. Loudly competing voices are raised every day, shouting opposing opinions, putting forth competing agendas, and summoning starkly different visions of a utopian or dystopian future. Often these voices attempt to shout the others down; there is precious little listening and considering among the cacophonous din. Yet listening and considering, too, are essential to the health of a democracy. If controversy is democracy's lusty lifeblood, respectful listening and careful thought are its higher faculties, its brain, its conscience.

Current Controversies does not shy away from or attempt to hush the loudly competing voices. It seeks to provide readers with as wide and representative as possible a range of articulate voices on any given controversy of the day, separates each one out to allow it to be heard clearly and fairly, and encourages careful listening to each of these well-crafted, thoughtfully expressed opinions, supplied by some of today's leading academics, thinkers, analysts, politicians, policy makers, economists, activists, change agents, and advocates. Only after listening to a wide range of opinions on an issue, evaluating the strengths and weaknesses of each argument, assessing how well the facts and available evidence mesh with the stated opinions and conclusions, and thoughtfully and critically examining one's own beliefs and conscience can the reader begin to arrive at his or her own conclusions and articulate his or her own stance on the spotlighted controversy.

This process is facilitated and supported in each Current Controversies volume by an introduction and chapter overviews that provide readers with the essential context they need to begin engaging with the spotlighted controversies, with the debates surrounding them, and with their own perhaps shifting or nascent opinions on them. Chapters are organized around several key questions that are answered with diverse opinions representing all points on the political spectrum. In its content, organization, and methodology, readers are encouraged to determine the authors' point of view and purpose, interrogate and analyze the various arguments and their rhetoric and structure, evaluate the arguments' strengths and weaknesses, test their claims against available facts and evidence, judge the validity of the reasoning, and bring into clearer, sharper focus the reader's own beliefs and conclusions and how they may differ from or align with those in the collection or those of classmates.

Research has shown that reading comprehension skills improve dramatically when students are provided with compelling, intriguing, and relevant "discussable" texts. The subject matter of these collections could not be more compelling, intriguing, or urgently relevant to today's students and the world they are poised to inherit. The anthologized articles also provide the basis for stimulating, lively, and passionate classroom debates. Students who are compelled to anticipate objections to their own argument and identify the flaws in those of an opponent read more carefully, think more critically, and steep themselves in relevant context, facts, and information more thoroughly. In short, using discussable text of the kind provided by every single volume in the Current Controversies series encourages close reading, facilitates reading comprehension, fosters research, strengthens critical thinking, and greatly enlivens and energizes classroom discussion and participation. The entire learning process is deepened, extended, and strengthened.

If we are to foster a knowledgeable, responsible, active, and engaged citizenry, we must provide readers with the intellectual, interpretive, and critical-thinking tools and experience necessary to make sense of the world around them and of the all-important debates and arguments that inform it. We must encourage them not to run away from or attempt to quell controversy but to embrace it in a responsible, conscientious, and thoughtful way, to sharpen and strengthen their own informed opinions by listening to and critically analyzing those of others. This series encourages respectful engagement with and analysis of current controversies and competing opinions and fosters a resulting increase in the strength and rigor of one's own opinions and stances. As such, it helps readers assume their rightful place in the public square and provides them with the skills necessary to uphold their awesome responsibility—guaranteeing the continued and future health of a vital, vibrant, and free democracy.

Introduction

> *"The environment and the economy*
> *are really both two sides of the*
> *same coin. If we cannot sustain the*
> *environment we cannot sustain*
> *ourselves."*
>
> —*Wangari Maathai*

The green economy is an economic system that prioritizes green energy, environmental preservation, and the reduction of pollution and carbon emissions. Contrary to the brown or fossil fuel–driven economy that serves as the default system, the green economy strives to improve social and environmental conditions along with economic growth. In a green economy infrastructure, development and other investments are all funneled into sustainable channels that also consider carbon emissions and the environment.

In the United States, as in most of the world, the economy is primarily driven by fossil fuels. This means our transportation, production, distribution, and consumption habits are powered by oil, coal, and gas. Beginning with the Industrial Revolution in the late eighteenth century, fossil fuels served as the easiest and cheapest way to expand economies through the creation of jobs and products and improve quality of life. This period is responsible for the dramatic increase in economic growth in the developed world. Unfortunately, it also marks the beginning of large-scale pollution and carbon emissions.

After the Paris Agreement of 2016, nations around the world agreed that tackling climate change and keeping temperatures from rising beyond 1.5 degrees Celsius was imperative. However, debate at the conference centered around responsibility for climate change and who would bear the burden of fixing it. The developed world is largely responsible for climate change, and nations in the developing world argue that they deserve the same chance to industrialize now that they are acquiring the infrastructure and capabilities required. In the end, a framework was developed to help developed countries assist with climate change mitigation in developing countries. Much of the world's oil and gas supply comes from nations still in the process of developing, thus switching to a green economy would be costly, difficult, and time consuming for these nations.

Many developing nations may still require fossil fuel–driven economies while they catch up on economic growth. However, economic growth is not only possible through the fossil fuel economy. The green economy provides ample opportunity for growth and development as well. For instance, switching to a green economy in the United States would require the large-scale installation of green energy, like solar and wind. This would create hundreds of thousands of new jobs, reduce our dependence on foreign oil, and revitalize the American consumer market with new products and services.

Social problem alleviation is also possible through the green economy. In addition to ensuring environmentally friendly growth, the green economy challenges issues of justice related to fueling society. The green economy removes human rights problems related to oil and gas extraction and works to enhance equity and inclusion. The Green New Deal, a legislative proposal related to the green economy in the United States, includes provisions on fair and equitable health care, education, housing, and safe water and air. Justice and well-being are just as much a part of the green economy as sustainability.

So, if the green economy is better for the environment, workers, and communities, why is it not our default economic system? Unfortunately, the green economy may not do enough to address climate change. The costs of switching economic models become greater considerations if the rewards are not what we expect them to be. Some argue that climate change has already escalated to such a dangerous level that even a green economy couldn't mitigate the problem. Others contend that the green economy lacks political and technical feasibility. Although legislation like the Green New Deal is popular among young people, politicians and other political actors are still reticent to give their support.

The viewpoints contained in *Current Controversies: Fossil Fuel Industries and the Green Economy* explore this debate and consider the history of green and brown economic systems. They also investigate the environmental and social impacts of these economies. Climate experts, political pundits, economic scholars, and everyday citizens consider the merits and difficulties of the green economy. Readers are challenged to consider the many facets of economic development and conclude whether the green economy is the right choice for our future.

CHAPTER 1

Is the Green Economy Financially Superior to the Fossil Fuel Economy?

Overview: Explaining the Green Economy

Manish Bapna and John Talberth

Manish Bapna serves as the executive vice president and oversees the research and the management team at the World Resources Institute. John Talberth is a writer at the World Resources Institute.

The global recession has brought new attention to chronic structural flaws in current economic models and assumptions. As economies struggle to recover, many are taking a closer look at the broad concept of a "Green Economy," one that simultaneously promotes sustainability and economic growth What would this type of economy look like, and how could we get there? WRI Managing Director Manish Bapna responds to some of the most commonly-asked questions:

What Is a Green Economy?

A Green Economy can be thought of as an alternative vision for growth and development; one that can generate growth and improvements in people's lives in ways consistent with sustainable development. A Green Economy promotes a triple bottom line: sustaining and advancing economic, environmental and social well-being.

The prevailing economic growth model is focused on increasing GDP above all other goals. While this system has improved incomes and reduced poverty for hundreds of millions, it comes with significant and potentially irreversible social, environmental and economic costs. Poverty persists for as many as two and a half billion people, and the natural wealth of the planet is rapidly being drawn down. In a recent global assessment, approximately 60 percent of the world's ecosystem services were found to be degraded or used unsustainably. The gap between the rich and poor is also increasing—between 1990 and 2005, income inequality (measured by the gap between the highest and lowest income earners) rose in more than two thirds of countries.

The persistence of poverty and degradation of the environment can be traced to a series of market and institutional failures that make the prevailing economic model far less effective than it otherwise would be in advancing sustainable development goals. These market and institutional failures are well known to economists, but little progress has been made to address them. For example, there are not sufficient mechanisms to ensure that polluters pay the full cost of their pollution. There are "missing markets"—meaning that markets do not systematically account for the inherent value of services provided by nature, like water filtration or coastal protection. A "market economy" alone cannot provide public goods, like efficient electricity grids, sanitation or public transportation. And economic policy is often shaped by those who wield power, with strong vested interests, and rarely captures the voice and perspectives of those most at risk.

A Green Economy attempts to remedy these problems through a variety of institutional reforms and regulatory, tax, and expenditure-based economic policies and tools.

What Does a Green Economy Look Like?

The transition to a Green Economy has a long way to go, but several countries are demonstrating leadership by adopting national "green growth" or "low carbon" economic strategies. And there are many examples of successful, large-scale programs that increase growth or productivity and do so in a sustainable manner. For example:

- The Republic of Korea has adopted a national strategy and a five-year plan for green growth for the period 2009–2013, allocating 2 percent of its gross domestic product to investment in several green sectors such as renewable energy, energy efficiency, clean technology and water. The government has also launched the Global Green Growth

Institute, which aims to help countries (especially developing countries) develop green growth strategies.

- In Mexico City, crippling congestion led to a major effort to promote Bus Rapid Transit (BRT), a sophisticated bus system that uses dedicated lanes on city streets. Significant public investment in the BRT has reduced commuting times and air pollution and improved access to public transit for those less able to afford private cars. This remarkable success is now being replicated in cities across Mexico and has led to investment from the federal government in urban public transit for the first time.

- China now invests more than any other country in renewable energy. Its total installed wind capacity grew 64 percent in 2010. This growth is driven by a national policy that sees clean energy as a major market in the near future, and one in which China wants to gain a competitive edge.

- Namibia is managing its natural resources to generate economic, social, and environmental benefits. Local communities across the country are granted the right to use and capitalize on the benefits of using wildlife and other natural resources within the boundaries of "communal conservancies." With an economic incentive to sustainably manage these areas, food and employment is being provided for hundreds of thousands of Namibians in rural areas. More than half of the jobs are filled by women, and wildlife populations have increased.

- Businesses are increasingly leading progress toward a Green Economy. For example, the carpet company Interface FLOR is improving its competitive positioning in this normally petroleum-intensive industry by focusing on how sustainability can enhance its business model. The company is working towards a closed loop system, meaning that its waste products are also its manufacturing inputs. Its company culture reinforces its goals—when employees know they are making a difference in the world, they tend to work harder and be better at their jobs, making the enterprise more productive. Interface's CEO, Ray Anderson, has said, "If we can do it, anyone can. And if anyone can, everyone can."

How Does a Green Economy Differ from Previous Efforts to Promote Sustainability—What Is New?

In many ways, Green Economy objectives simply support those already articulated for the broader goal of sustainable development. But this new framing responds to two recent developments.

First, there is a deeper appreciation today by many governments, companies, civil society and the public that we are reaching planetary limits, not just in terms of greenhouse gas emissions but also in our use of water, land, forests and other natural resources. The environmental and social costs of our current economic model are becoming more and more apparent.

Second, and perhaps even more important, the global recession has led to a reconsideration of key tenets of the current economic model—such as the primacy of growth and the belief in light-touch regulation. In openly questioning the strength of the status quo, many public- and private-sector leaders are seeking:

- Policies and regulations that can identify and manage financial and other risks more effectively
- New markets and industries that can create good, long-term jobs
- Public support for innovation to position a country to compete in tomorrow's markets

These developments point to the need for new sources of growth that are environmentally sustainable—for example, employment in high-growth sectors such as clean energy. Past sustainability efforts have not focused sufficiently on fixing the failures of economic policies such as pricing pollution. But we now have a chance to tackle these challenging problems given the policy openings created by the response to the financial crisis. A good example is Korea's adoption of a national green growth strategy (described above).

Some see marrying sources of new growth with sustainability as the future. Why is China investing in wind? To win tomorrow's markets, not necessarily to compete in today's. As the late C. K. Prahalad—a visionary on corporate strategy—was fond of saying, "We need to move from seeing sustainability as a cost or hindrance to realizing that it's a key driver of innovation."

What Are Some of the Concerns and Tensions with the Concept of a Green Economy?

One question people ask is "can we afford this?" We're still in the wake of the global financial crisis and many people perceive Green Economy solutions as expensive. The United States is asking itself whether it can afford to put a price on carbon today. Developing countries are concerned that transitioning to a Green Economy will hinder economic growth and the ability to reduce poverty.

Moreover, there will be short-term, nontrivial losses associated with changes in industry and market structure (e.g., a decline of the coal industry and related job losses). Supporting those actors who will bear the brunt of the transition will be critical to building broad ownership for a Green Economy.

Some countries feel that they are lagging in green technology know-how and therefore will be at a competitive disadvantage in the race for future markets. Others feel that the Green Economy is a pretense for rich countries to erect "green" trade barriers on developing country exports. These are all legitimate concerns that deserve attention.

Ultimately, a hard-nosed economic analysis should inform decisions on what policies and investments to promote today. When the full costs and benefits over time are taken into account, however, many Green Economy solutions will be seen as more attractive. Nevertheless, there will still be difficult choices and tradeoffs. For example, should India aggressively promote grid-connected, relatively expensive solar power when hundreds of millions in the country still have no access to electricity? And even where Green Economy solutions make economic sense, they may be politically challenging. The transition to a Green Economy will not be easy.

What Are the Challenges to a Transition to a Green Economy, and What Will Make It Possible?

The principal challenge is how we move towards an economic system that will benefit more people over the long run. Transitioning to a Green Economy will require a fundamental shift in thinking about growth and development, production of goods and services, and consumer habits. This transition will not happen solely because of better information on impacts, risks or good economic analysis; ultimately, it is about politics and changing the political economy of how big decisions are made.

The problem is vested interests. Those who benefit from the status quo are either overrepresented in or have greater access to institutions that manage natural resources and protect the environment. US climate legislation, for example, was defeated in no small part by resistance from fossil-fuel-based energy advocates.

The following steps would help create a more level policy-making playing field:

- Increase public awareness and the case for change. Greater visibility on the need for this transition can motivate voters and consumers—not just because of the costs but also the economic benefits generated by a Green Economy, such as new jobs and new markets. People will not adopt policies because they are green. They will do so when they believe it is in their interest.
- Promote new indicators that complement GDP. Planning agencies and finance ministries should adopt a more diverse and representative set of economic indicators that focus less exclusively on growth and track the pace and progress of development.
- Open up government decision-making processes to the public and civil society. This would help ensure policies

are accountable to the public and not to vested and well-connected interests.

- Identify and take advantage of political leadership when available as this will be crucial in order to limit the undue influence of "dirty" economic holdouts.

Timing is everything when it comes to big policy reforms. Green Economy advocates will need to be ready when that window of opportunity presents itself.

Ultimately, the widespread transition to a Green Economy will depend on whether or not the long-term public interest is reflected in today's economic policies.

Businesses Will Profit from the Green Economy

GlobeScan

GlobeScan is an international insights and strategy firm.

Businesses making the transition towards the green economy are already reaping rewards worth hundreds of millions of dollars in savings and high return on investment, while benefiting consumers, communities and the environment, says a new report entitled The Business Case for the Green Economy: Sustainable Return on Investment.

The report, produced by the UN Environment Programme (UNEP) in partnership with SustainAbility and GlobeScan, uses compelling economic and scientific data and a wide-ranging collection of real-life case studies to demonstrate the advantages of the green economy in action.

- Unilever's Sustainable Living Plan, which aims to integrate sustainability into business models, has led to savings of over US $10 million annually. At the same time, their "one rinse" washing formulas, which save an average of 30 litres per wash, are now used across 12.5 million households worldwide—a 60 per cent increase over 2010.
- Siemens produces half of the installed capacity of offshore wind turbines worldwide (2,000MW), saving about 4 million tonnes of CO_2 annually. It has recently announced investment of €150 million to offshore wind R&D and the expansion of its wind business.
- Grupo Bimbo in Mexico saved approximately US $700,000 and 338,400 m3 of water in 3 years through its water reduction programme.

"Businesses Cannot Afford to Ignore the Benefits of a Green Economy," GlobeScan Incorporated, June 16, 2012. Reprinted by permission.

- AVIVA, who launched its insurance product for Low-Carbon and Environmental Goods and Services in 2011, expects the sector to grow by an estimated UK £45 billion by 2015, supported by government decisions and financial incentives.
- PUMA conducted the first Environmental Porfit and Loss Account in 2010, in collaboration with Pricewaterhousecooper and Trucost. The value of environmental impact was calculated at €145 million (seen as negative financial impact). Using the tool allows PUMA to reduce future financial loss while strengthening its operating margin by taking into account emerging risks. The company committed itself to having 50 per cent of its products made from sustainable materials by 2015.
- In Egypt, SEKEM Group's compost project helped save more than 300,000 tonnes of CO_2 equivalents between 2007 and 2011 and increased sales from EGP 788,400 to over EGP 10.5 million in 2010.
- General Motors saved more than US $30 million in 6 years through their resource productivity programme. They also reduced waste volume by 40 per cent.
- In China, the Zhangzidao Fishery Group saw revenues grow by 40 per cent annually between 2005 and 2010 (compared to the industry's 13 per cent average) through offering an alternative to monoculture methods. The integrated Multi-Tropic Aquaculture approach employed by the company provided for a more balanced ecosystem, taking into account local conditions and environmental quality.
- The Colombian Coffee Growers Federation ensures a sustainable income for more than 27,000 coffee growers with its Rainforest Alliance certified coffee, as part of the Nespresso AAA Sustainable Quality™ program.
- Markets for biodiversity offsets are predicted to grow to US $10 billion by 2020.
- In the offshore wind sector alone, employment in Europe is projected to grow to 150,000 by 2020 and to over 200,000 by

2030, while global revenues for companies involved in the renewable energy markets are projected to rise to more than US $300 billion annually by 2020.

According to experts, companies investing in sustainable innovation to increase resource efficiency and responsible operations ahead of formal regulatory frameworks are achieving competitive advantage by positioning themselves to capture the mainstream markets of the next decade.

UN Under-Secretary General and UNEP Executive Director, Achim Steiner, said, "Business can no longer afford to ignore the benefits that switching to a Green economy will bring. Pioneers that are leading the market are reaping the rewards and positioning themselves for sustained success that benefits their customers and communities."

"Decoupling economic growth from environmental damage is required to prevent large scale economic as well as environmental impact. Rio+20 provides an unprecedented opportunity to scale-up and accelerate these efforts. As governments gather to consider future green economy frameworks, we invite business to step-up and show the role it can play in generating jobs, developing energy efficient technologies, in greening its supply chains and in integrating sound governance principles throughout their decision-making," he added.

From utility companies in emerging markets to consumer goods companies in developed markets, sustainable goods and services are moving from niche to the mainstream.

Paul Polman, Unilever's Chief Executive Officer, said, "At Unilever we see no conflict between sustainability and economic growth. We have to have both, and increasingly we see that one is not possible without the other. This new report from UNEP confirms this, with cases drawn not just from our own business but many others in a variety of sectors, exploring the ways in which sustainability reduces risk, generates cost savings, and creates opportunities for growth, providing the foundation for a new business model for the 21st century."

Leveraging Benefits

Research shows that the provision of sustainable products and services bolsters sales growth, market share, brand value and reputation, while increasing customer loyalty.

Jeff Erikson, Senior Vice President at SustainAbility and a contributor to the report, said, "In the 25 years we have worked on corporate sustainability, we have witnessed time and again the multiple ways that sustainability delivers business value to companies that adopt it as a strategic principle."

He added, "The companies currently leading the transition to the Green Economy realize it's not about bravery—it's about the bottom line."

There is strong evidence that in recent years demand for sustainable products has been resilient, with many customers willing to pay a premium for sustainability credentials.

A National Geographic/GlobeScan survey in 2010 found that consumers in Brazil, India and China scored the highest in terms of environmentally sustainable consumer behavior.

Other survey results show that in future business-to-business and business-to-consumer transactions, customers will expect all products to be environmentally and socially responsible.

The new lifestyle markets, markets for sustainable cities, the service markets, the organics and certified markets are all examples of opportunities to be cultivated and seized.

Financial institutions play a dual role in the transition towards a green economy through both investing in sustainable projects and integrating environmental, social and governance indicators (ESG) into the decision making criteria of their everyday operation—from lending to investment and insurance.

ESG performance is increasingly seen as a proxy for management quality; hence the growing interest on the part of businesses in sustainability rating schemed.

Experts estimate that the annual financing required to create the green economy is in the range of US $1-2.5 trillion. The investment represents an opportunity for the private sector to provide the infrastructure, equipment, goods and services that will drive the transition.

Business alone, however, cannot deliver the speed and scale of change required. Collaboration with regulators, customers and the financial community is essential.

Public policies linked to clear principles of sustained economic success are necessary to support this transition.

Preferable Taxation and Reduced Capital Cost

Improving tax regimes to award sustainable innovation is seen as an important incentive.

Locations with higher environmental standards and tax subsidies are more attractive to investors.

In Guatemala, tax breaks are provided on equipment for projects designed to support the goal of generating 60 per cent of electricity from hydro and geothermal sources by 2022.

The OECD has confirmed a growing movement towards environmental tax breaks and tradable permits in OECD economies over the last decade. The value of green taxes to boost innovation is evident through increased investment in research and development and registration of patents on new, cleaner technologies.

Other examples of national and city-level tax incentives for cleaner energy include:

- Brazil, Belo Horizonte: Tax credits for residential solar power.
- China: Subsidies on green cars and financing for the construction of infrastructure for charging electric cars across five cities.
- India: Carbon tax on local production.
- Zambia: Tax reductions in mining areas to stimulate investment in renewables.
- Argentina, Bolivia, Colombia, Spain, Belgium, France, UK, Greece, Ireland, USA, South Africa, Sweden, Slovenia, Lithuania, Italy: Fuel tax exemption in favour of biofuels.

Risk Profile and New Opportunities

According to the report, businesses that have effective environmental and social risk management systems in place are in a position to secure a better risk profile, thus enabling them to obtain capital at lower cost.

It indicates that climate change, for example, is opening up new opportunities for sustainable products and services in the finance sector.

For instance, there is a pressing need to increase the availability of capital to further develop insurance schemes against environmental risk.

Equity Bank of Kenya made profits of over Ksh12.8 billion in 2011 by providing loans at competitive interest rates to farmers who introduce environmental practices such as drip irrigation and water efficiency projects.

In addition to that, the bank's customer base reached Ksh7.15 million in the same year, making it the largest bank by consumer base in sub-Saharan Africa.

Overcoming Challenges

A survey of sustainability experts and practitioners—conducted by UNEP, GlobeScan and SustainAbility in 2011—examined the reasons why more businesses are not joining the race towards a green economy transition.

Results of the survey indicate that the majority of stakeholders perceived a disconnect between the stated political goals of sustainability and actual policies on the ground.

- An overwhelming 88 per cent of respondents cited the long-standing problem of financial short-termism as the most important barrier for developing sustainability-focused business models; with some investors exploiting the rise in demand—driven by resource scarcity—to push prices up.
- 65 per cent of respondents cited inefficient regulatory regimes as key barrier; referring to regulations that inhibit change,

combined with lack of regulation that encourages more sustainable practices.

- Similarly, 65 per cent of those surveyed indicated that the low level of awareness of the sustainability imperative among business leaders was a significant barrier.

If more business leaders and executives developed better understanding of the risks and opportunities that issues such as human rights, climate change, and water scarcity represented to their business, the pace of the transition would significantly increase.

The Lack of Formal International Standards Represented Another Barrier

International guidelines and standards such as the Global Reporting Initiative (GRI) and the ISO 26000 Social Responsibility Standards are being widely adopted by major corporations around the world, albeit on voluntary basis.

These leading businesses are now calling for mandatory social and environmental reporting to drive up performance and create fair market advantage.

The Way Forward: An Action Plan for Business

Experts recommend businesses adopt a set of transformative actions to help drive the transition to the green economy by:

- Driving policy change in support of responsible business investment.
- Encouraging stakeholder and employee engagement.
- Establishing sustainability as a core governance issue on the board agenda and communicate its value to investors and consumers.
- Enhancing resilience and business growth by adopting valuation techniques that go beyond monetary valuation to adequately capture the value of human, social and natural capital.

- Creating incentives and mechanisms to embed sustainability within the company's culture.

According to the report, the successful transition to the green economy over the long term will require new skills, diverse collaborations, continuous innovation, investment s with uncertain return and a change in market values.

Companies, like governments, will need to choose wisely if they are to capitalize on the opportunities ahead.

The gathering of leaders from government, business and civil society at the Rio+20 UN Conference on Sustainable Development presents a historic opportunity to accelerate the transition to a green economy. While public policy is an essential ingredient in making the green economy a reality, it is the actions of the private sector that will ultimately determine the pace and shape of the transition.

The Green Economy Makes Access to Electricity Possible for All

United Nations Environment Programme

The United Nations Environment Programme is the branch of the UN concerned with its environmental agenda and sustainable development.

The most dramatic and pervasive example of how we have come to dominate our planet is climate change, which the Intergovernmental Panel on Climate Change (IPCC) has unequivocally linked to CO_2 and greenhouse gas emissions from human activities. In its latest report, the IPCC warns that failure to reduce emissions could exacerbate food insecurity and result in the flooding of major cities and entire island nations. This could cause further refugee crises, mass extinction of plants and animals, and a drastically altered climate that might change life as we know it today for hundreds of millions of people.

All of these impacts are being propelled, to a large extent, by our current linear economic system: we extract, produce, consume, and discard. This has provided some with an opulent lifestyle, but continues to exact a great environmental toll on the planet. Further, the conventional thinking in the 20th century was that our fossil-fuel-dependent energy system would dominate well past the 21st century and underpin development in the world's poorest countries. We need to change, and we need to start by evolving our economic paradigm in terms of a transition to a green economy.

By this I mean an economy that improves human well-being and social equity while significantly reducing environmental risks and ecological scarcities. In its simplest expression, a green economy is low-carbon, resource-efficient, and socially inclusive.

"Evolution and the Green Economy in the Age of the Anthropocene," by United Nations Environment Programme, December 15, 2014. Reprinted by permission.

Practically speaking, a green economy is one in which growth in income and employment is driven by public and private investments that reduce carbon emissions and pollution, enhance energy and resource efficiency, and prevent the loss of biodiversity and the ecosystem services of clean air, clean water, and healthy soils.

Clean energy is not just a desirable element of the green economy, it is essential. The development and deployment of clean energy technologies in the past decade has been nothing short of astounding. No one, for example, imagined that between 2004 and 2011, 70% of new power capacity added in Europe would come from renewable energy sources.

At its core, the evolution of clean energy is a logical consequence based on quickly evolving technologies that are redefining the DNA of our energy systems—from the simple viral extraction and combustion of fossil fuels to the double helix of energy efficiency and renewable energy.

The concept of clean energy has now spread to every corner of the globe, replacing the traditional thinking that said our economic future needs fossil fuels, particularly for developing economies. From dirty to clean, and from limited to renewable—we now know it is no longer necessary and increasingly unprofitable to support technologies that damage the atmosphere and biosphere when so many cost-effective and cleaner solutions exist today.

The Facts Are Powerful and Often Surprising

In 2013, the electricity sector added more new renewable capacity than fossil-fueled and nuclear capacity combined. By 2030, new renewable capacity, including large-scale hydro, could exceed new thermal capacity by seven times, without even counting cogeneration.

One of the most surprising trends is the growth of micropower— sources of electricity that are relatively small, modular, mass-producible, quick to deploy, and rapidly scalable. Their capital cost, deployment times, and carbon footprint are the opposite of large-scale fossil-fueled power plants that often cost billions of dollars and can take up to a decade to license and build.

Micropower includes renewable energy technologies, other than big hydroelectric dams, and cogeneration of electricity together with useful heat in factories or buildings (also known as combined heat and power, or CHP).

The startling fact is that micropower now produces about one-fourth of the world's total electricity. In its 2014 Solar Roadmap publication, the International Energy Agency (IEA) notes that micropower based on off-grid solar systems is now "the most suitable solution for minimum electrification" in sparsely populated rural areas. With proper financing to manage high initial costs, the IEA report says that by 2030, around 500 million people of the current 1.3 billion people with no access to electricity could enjoy the equivalent of 200W of solar PV capacity. This would be equivalent to 100GW of solar generation, not far short of the total solar PV deployment to date, and would be entirely in mini-grid and off-grid situations.

Another important trend is better energy storage. Citigroup estimates a 240GW global market for energy storage worth more than $400 billion by 2030. Its report Energy Darwinism II notes that the global energy mix is shifting more rapidly than is widely appreciated, and this has major implications for power generators, utilities and consumers, as well as for exporters of fossil fuels. Combined with electric vehicles, for example, new energy storage options integrated into smart grids could eliminate the need for peaking power plants.

The transition to a clean energy economy—a green economy— is under way. But sooner is not just better; it will also be cheaper, particularly in terms of global warming and climate change.

In UNEP's recent publication *The Clean Energy Voyage*, many examples already indicate that the "destination" of a clean energy economy is already being realized at the local, regional, state and national levels. Examples from China, Morocco, Brazil, Kenya, Nicaragua and South Africa demonstrate the capacity and pace with which developing economies are seizing the opportunity of renewables. And from Denmark and Iceland to Tuvalu, San Francisco and 60 cities and regions in Germany, a growing "Club 100" demonstrates how it is possible to move to an economy based on 100 per cent sustainable energy now.

One of the most significant actions governments can take is to simply remove or redirect subsidies for mature and profitable fossil fuels—a figure estimated to be $600 billion annually, according to the IEA. Combined with a new climate agreement in 2015, the transition to a green economy can be realized more quickly than most imagine today, but only if we direct the estimated $37 trillion that will be invested in energy infrastructure and projects over the coming two decades into accelerating and scaling up clean energy technologies.

As Victor Hugo observed, nothing is as powerful as an idea whose time has come. A green economy based on renewable energy and energy efficiency is just such an idea, and its arrival could very well determine whether the "Anthropocene" will be an age in which human ingenuity and responsibility will allow 10 billion people to have access to electricity without compromising the vital life support systems of our planet.

The Rise of the Green Economy

United Nations Framework Convention on Climate Change

The United Nations Framework Convention on Climate Change is the branch of the UN that aims to reduce greenhouse gas emissions.

According to a report by FTSE Russell, a key provider of stock market indices and associated data, the green economy is now worth as much as the fossil fuel sector and offers more significant and safe investment opportunities, pointing towards even more significant growth in the future.

The green economy is defined as an economy that aims at reducing environmental risks and ecological scarcities, and that aims for sustainable development without degrading the environment.

The green economy is also characterized by being efficient, clean, circular, collaborative and low carbon. As such, it is central to achieving the key objective of the Paris Agreement on climate action.

Presently, the green economy is worth as much as the fossil fuel sector with 6% of the global stock market, roughly $4 trillion USD, coming from the clean energy, energy efficiency, water, waste and pollution services.

If the sustainable economy maintains its current course, it could represent as much as 10% of the global market value by 2030, assuming around $90 USD trillion in green investment have been made by then.

FTSE Russel found that, over the last five years, green companies generated higher returns than the broader stock market. The report finds large investment opportunity, backed by global efforts to combat climate change and broader environmental challenges.

"Green Economy Overtaking Fossil Fuel Industry—FTSE Russel Report," by United Nations Framework Convention on Climate Change, June 8, 2018.

"Climate change is the death of progress and prosperity. Doing nothing about it is simply a bad investment in the future," said UN Climate Chief Patricia Espinosa in a message to the World Manufacturing Convention in China earlier this year. "The shape of the new economy is clear: it's clean, green and prosperous, and I encourage all of you to get on board," she added.

The FTSE Russel report finds the green economy has spread across companies of various size, nature, and geographical range in contrast to fossil fuels, which has shrunk. Still, more work is required to keep the global economy on track to meet the Paris agreement goals.

The report analyzes a broad range of products and services from different sectors. Findings were based on the impact of these factors on climate change mitigation and adaptation, water, resource use, pollution, and agricultural efficiency.

In terms of diversification, large companies lead the way by representing roughly two thirds of the total green market value. Similarly, small and medium sized firms now represent a larger number of green companies.

The energy industry, a very diverse segment ranging from building insulation to cloud technology, makes up more than half of the green economy with food, agriculture, water and transport being other important sectors.

Specifically, the buildup of cloud infrastructure technology is a focus for industry leaders such as Microsoft and Amazon. According to a recent Accenture report, companies can reduce carbon emissions by up to 90% by switching to cloud computing technology.

Alternative energy also plays a significant role in rapidly growing and diversifying solar and more established technologies, such as large hydroelectric. Resources such as lithium for batteries, lightweight materials, organic foods or seeds developed to boost agricultural yields are also a key area of the green economy.

Moreover, the study found approximately 3,000 globally listed companies with exposure to the green economy. This number has risen by approximately 20% since 2009 and covers 30% of global listed market value.

The largest companies in the green economy are a mix of both companies where the majority of their revenue is green, such as Tesla or Waste Management Inc, and large companies where a segment is green, such as Microsoft or Siemens.

The report allows investors to understand their interactions with the green economy while developing investment strategies by quantitatively measuring the world's transition to sustainability.

Transformational decarbonization is happening across the world in all sectors resulting from technological innovation, new and creative policies and political will at all levels.

The Global Climate Action Summit, which will take place from September 12-14 in California, is the next big opportunity for businesses to provide confidence to governments to "step up" ambition to achieve the goals of the Paris Agreement, and we can expect a further strengthening of the green economy at that event, co-chaired by Patricia Espinosa as the UN's top climate change official.

Constraints of the Green Economy

Barbara Unmüßig, Lili Fuhr, and Thomas Fatheuer

Barbara Unmüßig and Lili Fuhr are the president and head of the International Environmental Policy Division at the Heinrich Böll Foundation, respectively. Thomas Fatheuer is a former director of the foundation's Rio de Janeiro office and a social scientist.

In recent years, the push to build a "green economy" that can deliver the world from continual environmental and economic crisis and usher in a new era of sustainable growth has been gathering force.

But the push has been a source of unexpected controversy, with many predicting little more than business as usual with a coat of green paint. Will reconciling environmental and economic imperatives be harder than we think?

In a word, yes. The mainstream perception is that the green economy will enable us to break free from our dependence on fossil fuels, without sacrificing growth. Many argue that the shift to a green economy can even spur new growth. But, as appealing as this idea is, it is not realistic, as we show in our new book *Inside the Green Economy.*

To be sure, it is possible for a genuinely "green" economy to be prosperous. But the model that prevails today focuses on quick and easy solutions. Moreover, it reasserts the primacy of economics, thereby failing to recognize the depth of the transformation that is required.

Instead of rethinking our economies with a view to adapting their functioning to environmental limits and imperatives, today's green economy seeks to redefine nature, in order to adapt it to existing economic systems.

"The Limits to Green Growth," by Barbara Unmüßig, Lili Fuhr, and Thomas Fatheuer, Project Syndicate, July 1, 2016. Reprinted by permission.

We now attach a monetary value to nature and add it to our balance sheets, with the protection of "natural capital," such as ecosystem services, offsetting environmental degradation, gauged by the global abstract currency of carbon metrics.

New market-based mechanisms, such as the trading of biodiversity credits, exemplify this approach. None of this prevents the destruction of nature; it simply reorganizes that destruction along market lines.

As a result of this narrow approach, current conceptions of the green economy have so many blind spots that the entire enterprise should be regarded as largely a matter of faith. The most powerful talisman is technological innovation, which justifies simply waiting for a cure-all invention to come along.

But, though new ideas and innovations are obviously vital to address complex challenges, environmental or otherwise, they are neither automatic nor inevitable.

Innovation, particularly technological innovation, is always shaped by its protagonists' interests and activities, so it must be judged in its social, cultural, and environmental context. If the relevant actors are not working to champion transformative technologies, the results of innovation can reinforce the status quo, often by extending the life of products and systems that are not fit to address society's needs.

Consider the automotive industry. Though it produces increasingly fuel-efficient engines, it puts them in larger, more powerful, and heavier vehicles than ever before, eating up efficiency gains through the so-called "rebound effect."

And it faces the temptation to spend more energy learning to manipulate emissions readings, as Volkswagen did, than on developing genuinely "green" vehicles.

Biofuels are not the answer, either. In fact, the use of biomass wreaks ecological and social havoc in developing economies, while de facto extending the lifetime of an obsolete combustion technology.

Clearly, the automotive industry cannot be blindly trusted to spearhead the radical reorganization, away from private vehicles, that is needed in the transport sector. And that is exactly the point. If we are to decouple economic growth from energy consumption and achieve real resource efficiency in a world of nine billion, much less ensure justice for all, we cannot let the economy lead the way.

Instead, we must view the green transformation as a political task. Only a political approach can manage, through genuinely representative institutions, differences of opinion and interest, guided by the kind of open debate, engaging civil society, that is vital to a pluralistic democracy.

Of course, not all countries are pluralistic democracies. In many that aren't (and even in some that claim to be), those who campaign for a more socially, economically, and ecologically equitable world face severe repression.

If they are to fulfill their indispensable role in driving forward the transformation that is needed, democratic countries must put respect for basic human rights, such as freedom of speech and peaceful assembly, at the top of their foreign-policy agendas.

These basic rights are the normative foundation upon which transformative strategies will have to be negotiated.

After all, the biggest obstacle to the socio-ecological transformation that the world needs is not, in the end, technological; much of what is required, from organic farming to networked mobility systems that don't rely on private vehicles, is already within reach.

The real problem is the lack of political will to implement and scale up those innovations opposed by vested economic interests. The challenge is thus to overcome these minority interests and ensure the protection of the broader public good—a task that is often left to civil society.

Some might argue that calling for radical transformation, rather than incremental change, is inappropriate. At a time when the world faces so many pressing challenges, from economic stagnation to political upheaval to massive refugee flows, any progress toward sustainability should be viewed as a victory. Pragmatic, politically feasible solutions to the environmental crisis should be celebrated, not criticized.

But this view implicitly underestimates the seriousness of the environmental crisis that the world faces, and assumes linear change when the needed transformation will be non-linear.

While some features of the green economy—resource conservation, the transition to renewable energies, specific technological innovations, and effective economic incentives, such as taxes—are undeniably important, they do not add up to the large-scale change needed to protect the interests of present and future generations.

The task that the world's democracies face today is to continue the project of modernity, embracing the latest knowledge about planetary boundaries, while advancing broad democratic participation and reducing poverty and social injustice.

This is no small undertaking, and requires passion and tenacity. But it is not beyond our capacity. The first step is to recognize the constraints that the "green economy" places on thought and action.

Expanding the Green Economy Is Expensive and Detrimental to Poor Communities

Katie Tahuahua

Katie Tahuahua is a communications director at the Texas Public Policy Foundation. She has written for several news outlets, including the Washington Examiner.

A new study confirms what conservatives have long suspected: Expensive climate change programs, such as the Green New Deal, would hurt the poor the most.

Researchers from the Euro-Mediterranean Center for Climate Change estimate that if every country participating in the Paris Climate Accord actually fulfilled its greenhouse gas emission reduction pledges, more than 3 million people will be pushed into poverty. That's on top of the 1 billion people around the world who still don't have electricity or any of the benefits that come with it—like clean running water, refrigeration, modern medical care, and home heating.

Reliable, affordable energy has the power to lift people from poverty. Making that energy less accessible is a disservice to both the less fortunate and to the environment.

History has shown that economic prosperity and environmental quality go hand in hand. Though the environmentalist Left loves to hate fossil fuels, our air and water are cleaner than ever because of them. The EPA's six key airborne pollutants, including lead and ozone, are down 74% since 1970—the cleanest on record. Scientific advancements, fueled by affordable energy and a thriving free market, have made our businesses more efficient and improved environmental technology.

Meanwhile, the green groups' claims that fighting climate change equals fighting economic inequality doesn't hold weight.

"Expensive Climate Change Programs Hurt the Poor Most," by Katie Tahuahua, *Washington Examiner*, August 13, 2019. Reprinted by permission.

Though it's impossible to truly quantify the cost of a proposal as expansive and vague as the Green New Deal, one new report estimates that implementing Rep. Alexandria Ocasio-Cortez's pièce de résistance will cost up to $100,000 per household in the first year alone. That $100,000 isn't the government's money; it comes from the taxpayers who will also feel the strain on their wallets from higher electricity and fuel costs.

No country, state, or city has ever achieved 100% renewable energy, or even close, and costs have invariably gone up under programs attempting to force a switch to wind and solar. Paying more for energy doesn't just mean a higher utility bill—those costs also balloon the price of essentially every transaction we could ever make. Living a safe, healthy, and comfortable life requires electricity, as does running a business.

When polled about climate change, Americans consistently say they aren't willing to pay more to stave off the supposed watery doomsday on the horizon. An AP poll found that well over two-thirds of Americans wouldn't consider paying just $10 more a month on their electricity bills. An even more damning poll in San Antonio, one of over 400 cities pledging to implement their own versions of the Paris accords, revealed more than half aren't willing to pay a single penny.

It's not that Americans don't care about the environment; despite this poll data, climate change consistently ranks as a major policy concern. They recognize the costs simply aren't worth strangling our economy and our quality of life.

The global reductions in greenhouse gas emissions proposed by the Paris Climate Accord, however unrealistic, are projected to reduce the temperature in 2100 by at most 0.17°. If we stop the temperature from rising two tenths of a degree but subject millions more people to poverty, will it have been worth it?

Protecting and preserving our natural environment should be a priority. But raging against climate change at the expense of human lives is no more than a pyrrhic victory.

The widespread adoption of fossil fuels coincides with the most rapid improvements in quality of life in recorded history, including life expectancy, hunger, education, infant mortality, child labor, economic freedom, gross domestic product, and more. The best path forward is to allow America to continue embracing our abundant, reliable, affordable energy to lift people here and abroad from poverty.

Politicians who claim their expensive environmental programs will solve economic injustice should take another look at the numbers.

The Green Economy Performs Poorly in Economic Models

James Barrett

James Barrett is a writer and the chief economist at the Clean Economy Development Center.

E conomics is critical to getting decent climate legislation passed, as Nobel Prize-winning economist Paul Krugman discusses in a extended piece for the *New York Times*. Economists like me have always suspected that this was true, but then we also suspect that economics is critical to pretty much everything. The problem is that economics hates the environment, or at least environmental policy.

In the real world, environmental policy has been very good for the economy. But economic analyses of climate legislation find that pollution limits slow economic growth and increase costs. The Waxman-Markey climate bill—the American Clean Energy Security Act (ACES)—is a perfect example. As any good wonk will tell you, the economic analyses of ACES actually looked pretty good, especially when compared to some of the econolyptic predictions of past climate policy. The problem is that while the analyses were pretty good for ACES, they were horrible for climate policy. The analysis done by the EPA was the source of some the lowest cost estimates that anyone put out. This analysis was actually bad news.

The reason why this is such bad news for climate policy is because it resonates strongly with people's fears, it reinforces the conventional wisdom that climate policy will hurt the economy, and because it's wrong.

The heart of the problem is that the economic models economists use were written, for the most part, by economists. They are based on logical economic theories that make sense to economists because, in part, they assume that everyone

"The Problem with a Green Economy: Economics Hates the Environment," by James Barrett, Grist Magazine, Inc., April 9, 2010. Reprinted by permission.

understands that economics is critical to pretty much everything, and act rationally as a result. Not "rational" in the sense that people understand the difference between up and down, but rational in the sense that if your boss cut your hourly wage, you would voluntarily choose to work fewer hours, even if you have a family to feed. If you take the assumptions that underlie economic rationality to their logical conclusions, they can result in a pretty strange view of the world and how it works:

Some Fallacies of Conventional Climate Economics

We Already Live in an Economically Optimal World

In an economically rational world, there is no inefficiency and everyone is investing the optimal amount of money on research and development of new technologies. If a business could save money by switching to a more efficient heating and cooling system, it would have done it already. Likewise, firms are investing in energy efficiency research up to the point where an additional dollar of investment yields an expected return of one dollar in energy savings. To do less would leave money on the table, and to do more would be a waste. Anything else would be irrational. The implication of this is that, with everyone constantly and correctly optimizing their behavior, there is nothing the government can do to make us any better off. If everyone is investing exactly the right amount in energy efficiency, government incentives for to do more would induce people to do too much, diverting resources from other areas with a higher rate of return. This assumption is most prevalent in what are called "general equilibrium" (GE) models. As you might guess, GE models are preferred by the economic profession, yielding logically consistent if demonstrably wrong results.

There Can Be No Win-Win Solutions

Since everyone is constantly optimizing their energy decisions, anything that could cut carbon emissions while simultaneously saving money or increasing profits has already been done. Emissions cuts that save money have, in economics terms, a negative price. Since no one would ever give you something you wanted and pay you for the privilege of taking it (that would be irrational even to most non-economists, I think), negative cost emissions reductions can't exist. While it might sound trivial, there is also a technical problem with this. Economic models have a hard time assimilating prices with a negative sign in front of them. So, we declare win-win solutions non-existent by fiat. The EPA analysis comes out looking so good for ACES in large part because the costs of carbon abatement are lower than in other models. But what if someone, say a big consulting firm (McKinsey & Company), went out into the real world and found that carbon abatement costs look more like this:

All those negative cost (win-win) emission reduction opportunities on the left of the McKinsey cost curve are essentially excluded from the EPA analysis—and CBO, EIA, NAM/ACCF … So even the most optimistic analysis of the bunch badly overstates the costs of cutting carbon. No doubt that some of these negative cost reductions require some effort to capture, which is what policy is for.

No One Ever Learns
One thing that has bedeviled economists for a while is how to approximate what we call "induced technical change," the technical advances that occur because of policy changes or in response to price changes. If energy prices go up, you would expect that people would look for new ways to use less energy, resulting in innovations of various kinds. This makes common sense, but figuring out how it all works in the context of an economic model turns out to be pretty tricky. One attempt at this was to use the idea of "learning by doing"—the idea that the more you use of something the more efficient you get at using it. That's great, except when you plug it into a model along with a climate policy, the climate policy causes you to use less energy, and the less you use of something the less efficient you get at using it. The end result was that carbon pricing

slowed innovation in carbon efficient technologies. Back to the drawing board.

Put all these together with the difficulty of parameterizing the global economy, along with a few more that get even wonkier (like how to value ecosystem loss a hundred years down the road), and the odds of getting things right starts to fall pretty rapidly. What's worse is that almost all of these problems bias the models' results in the same direction: toward higher economic costs of meeting any given reduction target.

Good News and Bad News

The good news is that there are a few people working to set the record straight. I've done some work of my own on this, basically forcing a model to understand the returns to investing in efficiency. The good people at ACEEE are always on the leading edge of research on energy efficiency and have done some very good work recently on laying out the case for why and how economic models should be improved. The E3 network of economists has some excellent work related to this as well.

The bad news is that the really good work is badly outnumbered. So when Congress and other people look at the literature and see it dominated by the bad or merely unhelpful, they naturally tend to discount the other stuff as outliers, as exemplified by how the Congressional Budget Office reinforced incorrect conventional wisdom with its analysis of climate policy. The CBO basically took an average of some of the existing (flawed) work in the field and used it as their basis for figuring out the macroeconomic costs, giving the conventional wisdom an implicit stamp of approval that it doesn't deserve. As a friend of mine once said: If you're a physicist and you come up with a new theory that turns the orthodox on its head, they give you a Nobel Prize. If you're an economist, they deny you tenure.

CHAPTER 2

Does the Green Economy Benefit Communities?

Overview: Risks and Rewards of the Fossil Fuel Economy

James Cust, David Manley, and Giorgia Cecchinato

James Cust serves as an economist at the World Bank. David Manley is a senior economic analyst at the Natural Resource Governance Institute. Giorgia Cecchinato is a research associate at the Natural Resource Governance Institute.

To achieve climate change goals, the world must cut consumption of fossil fuels dramatically. But climate change success may put developing countries rich in fossil fuels in an almost no-win situation.

If there is no progress in combating climate change, poor countries are likely to be disproportionately harmed by the floods, droughts, and other weather-related problems spawned by a warming planet. But if there are successful global actions to address climate change, poorer countries that are rich in fossil fuels will likely face a precipitous fall in the value of their coal, gas, and oil deposits. If the world makes a permanent move away from using fossil fuels, the likely result will be a huge reduction in the value of their national and natural wealth.

These nations face three special challenges. First, they have a higher proportion of their national wealth at risk than do wealthier countries and on average more years of reserves than major oil and gas companies. Second, they have limited ability to diversify their economies and sources of government revenues—and it would take them longer to do so than countries less dependent on fossil fuel deposits.

Last, economic and political forces in many of these countries create pressure to invest in industries, national companies, and

"Unburnable Wealth of Nations," by James Cust, David Manley, and Giorgia Cecchinato, *Finance and Development*, March 2017, Vol. 54, No. 1. © International Monetary Fund. Reprinted with permission.

projects based on fossil fuels—in essence doubling down on the risk and exacerbating the ultimate consequences of a decline in demand for their natural resources.

Carbon Risk

What seems clear to virtually all scientists who study the issue is that the world cannot consume all of its oil, gas, and coal reserves without catastrophic climate consequences. To limit the increase in global temperature to 2 degrees Celsius—the more conservative of the goals agreed to by governments at the 2015 climate change talks in Paris—more than two-thirds of current known reserves, let alone those yet to be discovered, must remain in the ground (IEA 2012). They are the indirect target of climate policies that seek to limit carbon emissions—probably through taxes and quotas on carbon and the fostering of new low-carbon technologies. At some point, therefore, it is likely that the market for fossil fuels, especially highly polluting coal, will dramatically shrink, and with it their value to exporting countries. Reserves—that is, so-called proven reserves, which are estimated to be extracted profitably at current prices—may also remain undeveloped if governments impose policies to limit the market supply of fossil fuel resources. For example, Collier and Venables propose a sequenced closing of the global coal industry (2014). Furthermore, unless there are major—and unlikely—breakthroughs in technology to capture the carbon emitted by fossil fuels, the sharply reduced demand for oil, gas, and coal will be permanent.

Such a "carbon market risk" is potentially catastrophic for the economies of low- and middle-income countries rich in fossil fuels. While many of them have enjoyed the benefits of fossil fuel extraction, including the significant excess profits sometimes associated with oil and gas exports, they have typically failed to diversify their economies. Those that discovered their fossil fuels more recently may find themselves arriving "too late to the party."

For these countries, carbon market risk highlights three vulnerabilities:

Fossil-Fuel-Rich Developing Countries Are Generally Highly Exposed to a Shrinking Market for Oil, Natural Gas, and Coal

A fall in fossil fuel prices for producers significantly reduces the excess profits available from fossil fuel extraction on existing investments and makes further development of reserves less profitable. If those reserves stay in the ground, future government revenues from fossil fuel extraction will be reduced as will other benefits to the domestic economy, such as job creation. Because fuel reserves are such a significant portion of their national wealth, these countries are more at risk if there is a permanent decline in prices than their richer counterparts and those less endowed with fossil fuel wealth. These countries have a median ratio of fossil fuel reserves to GDP of 3.6—which means the national wealth held in these reserves is valued at more than three-and-a-half times their total economic output. Lower demand for oil and gas would drain critical revenues that governments could spend on investments in health, education, and infrastructure. Further, fossil fuel exports are often a key source of government cash—accounting for over 50 percent of government budgets in the top 15 oil- and gas-producing countries between 2006 and 2010 (Venables 2016).

Struggle to Diversify Assets

Fossil-fuel-rich developing countries may be less able to diversify their assets away from this exposure than developed economies or fossil fuel companies. Whether they can diversify or reduce their wealth exposure to carbon market risk depends on how long it takes and how much it costs to convert fossil-fuel-related assets into other nonrelated assets and whether the economy can develop other strong productive sectors.

Analysts have warned that carbon market risk could strand the assets of fossil fuel companies (Leaton 2013), but countries are more vulnerable than private companies. Not only is it more difficult for countries to shift capital and capabilities into renewable energy technologies or other activities than it is for companies, countries are tied, geographically and constitutionally, to ownership of reserves, which cannot be sold outright but only licensed to companies for development. Unlike many fossil-fuel-rich developing countries, companies hold the development rights to relatively few reserves—and those have relatively high production rates. For example, in 2013, the reserve-to-production ratios for all oil and gas companies were 12.8 years and 13.9 years, respectively (EY 2013). Companies could, if they wanted, run down their existing reserves in less than 15 years.

Fossil-fuel-rich developing countries hold oil, gas, and coal assets that are harder to turn into cash—typically they can be converted into other assets only after the countries develop, produce, and sell fuel. Using past reserve-to-production ratios as a guide, we found that, unless they can find ways to significantly increase their rates of production, most countries must wait 45 years on average to liquidate their fossil fuel wealth.

Because it is difficult to develop new sources of national wealth, few resource-rich governments have successfully diversified their revenue streams. Moreover, their ability to use fossil fuel revenue to invest in foreign nonfuel assets—for example, through sovereign wealth funds—has been limited by the rate at which they can extract their reserves and the pressure to spend rather than save revenues. Consequently, the assets of sovereign wealth funds owned by governments of fossil-fuel-rich developing countries represent on average only 3 percent of the value of their fossil fuel reserves.

Political Pressure
Domestic political pressure to develop fossil fuel reserves pushes these countries into choices that might increase their exposure to carbon market risk. First, national oil companies, common in oil-rich countries, often involve state investment in fossil fuel assets for reasons other than maximizing revenue. If the expected life of these assets is so long that declining oil, gas, or coal prices will affect returns, or a government cannot liquidate them at a reasonable value, then governments that invest now in a national oil company—especially one intended to operate abroad—may be

exposing national wealth and public assets to carbon market risk (for example, the significant amount of state ownership in some of the largest national oil companies of fossil-fuel-rich developing countries). Second, policies to promote domestic participation in supply chains that process and/or transport fossil fuels may expose a country to carbon market risk by increasing the total share of a country's assets vulnerable to a decline in fossil fuel demand. Finally, fossil-fuel-rich countries have tended to develop economies that use a lot of carbon-based products. Research shows that petroleum and coal producers emit a significantly larger amount of carbon per dollar of GDP than countries that produce neither petroleum nor coal. A major reason is that the fossil-fuel-rich countries tend to subsidize consumption of fuels, such as gasoline (Friedrichs and Inderwildi 2013).

Policy Prospects

There are four policy implications arising from this carbon market risk that governments of fossil-fuel-rich developing countries should consider.

Diversification of Economy

The first is that diversification of the economy is more important than ever. This means countries should expand nonfuel sectors of the economy, especially alternative export sectors, such as manufacturing and agricultural processing, and certain services, such as information and communication technology. But it also means the tax base must be widened to wean the government off dependence on fossil fuel revenues.

Moreover, because it is not only reserves that become endangered by falling prices and demand, governments need to reconsider all their energy-related investments. State-owned companies and energy-related infrastructure and investments to enable the country to participate in supply chains may also fail to provide a sufficient return to the country if the world reduces its use of fossil fuels. Governments may wish to limit investment in these areas.

Some value of local businesses may decline, and a workforce specialized in fossil fuel extraction may become obsolescent. If local suppliers and labor can relatively easily adapt to changed circumstances and participate in supply chains outside the fossil fuel sector without protection or subsidies, a country may be able to benefit from educating workers in the fossil fuel sector. However, if training workers or building company capability to supply the fossil fuel sector takes decades—and if these skills and products are not transferable to other industries—not only will state capital invested in this effort be wasted, but so may the human capital that the workers and firms represent.

Promotion of Fossil Fuel Sectors

Second, governments should continue to promote the competitiveness of their fossil fuel sectors so long as they moderate public investment in these sectors. This may seem counterintuitive, but by reducing the costs investors face, it may be possible to mitigate the stranding of reserves by remaining an attractive destination for production. Studies suggest that oil and gas development is determined not only by geography but also by the quality of a country's political institutions, such as openness to foreign investors, the fairness of its judicial system (which reduces the threat of expropriation), and the ease of doing business (Cust and Harding 2015; Arezki, Toscani, and van der Ploeg 2016).

Although the world may have more reserves than can be safely burned, it does not follow that exploration should stop entirely in the lowest-income countries. Development and extraction are costly, but costs vary significantly across different geology, so it may be worthwhile for certain countries to allow exploration for reserves that may be less expensive to extract, even after a carbon tax is factored in.

Avoid Subsidies

Third, governments should avoid subsidizing fossil fuel use and the fossil fuel sector. Subsidies on the production side—either explicit, such as tax breaks, or implicit, such as poorly negotiated deals that reduce the tax burden of companies—may encourage too much exploration or extraction and keep the country dependent on fossil fuels for too long.

Consumption subsidies, such as on gasoline, might make other sectors of the economy (transportation, for example) more dependent on fossil fuels, reduce consumer incentives to drive less and use more-efficient forms of transportation—such as railroads or mass transit—or encourage investment related to fossil fuel consumption, such as highways.

Consider Pace

Fourth, governments and citizens should carefully consider whether to extract faster, slower, or not at all. The right answer may be different for different countries, but the danger of being "last to the party" may encourage some countries to promote exploration in the hope of realizing extraction revenues before climate policies or new technologies fully kick in.

However, Stevens, Lahn, and Kooroshy (2015) argue that for low-income countries, a slower pace of licensing may give the government time to upgrade institutions and potentially earn more future income by reducing investor risk and improving negotiating capacity. Further, even if faster development is an optimum strategy for one country, if all producers do the same thing, supply may rise and prices fall, a result known as the "green paradox" (van der Ploeg and Withagen 2015).

While still highly uncertain, there is a growing likelihood that fossil fuel consumption overall will decline. This is indicated not only by the outcome of the Paris climate change talks, but by emerging evidence that global economic activity is using less carbon per dollar of GDP and by the promise of technological breakthroughs in alternative energy sources such as solar and wind power. This creates the risk of "stranded nations" whose vast fossil fuel reserves are no longer worth extracting. It is unclear when, or by how much, this stranding will occur. But for policymakers in fossil-fuel-rich developing economies, stuck between the effects of a warming planet and global action to prevent such warming, how to deal with declining demand for their resources will be an ever more critical question and will call for new policy approaches. These countries should seek to harness the moment to develop other sectors of the economy rather than wait for the next commodity price boom.

Resources

1. Arezki, Rabah, Frederik G. Toscani, and Frederick van der Ploeg. 2016. "Shifting Frontiers in Global Resource Wealth." CEPR Discussion Paper DP11553, Centre for Economic Policy Research, London.

2. Collier, Paul, and Anthony J. Venables. 2014. "Closing Coal: Economic and Moral Incentives." *Oxford Review of Economic Policy* 30 (3): 492–512.

3. Cust, James, and Torfinn Harding. 2015. "Institutions and the Location of Oil Exploration." OxCarre Research Paper Series 127, Oxford University Centre for the Analysis of Resource Rich Countries, Oxford, United Kingdom.

4. EY. 2013. "Global Oil and Gas Reserves Study." London.

5. Friedrichs, Jörg, and Oliver Inderwildi. 2013. "The Carbon Curse: Are Fuel Rich Countries Doomed to High CO2 Intensities?" Energy Policy 62: 1356–65.

6. International Energy Agency (IEA). 2012. World Energy Outlook. Paris.

7. Leaton, James. 2013. "Unburnable Carbon 2013—Wasted Capital and Stranded Assets." Carbon Tracker Initiative, London.

8. McGlade, Christopher, and Paul Ekins. 2015. "The Geographical Distribution of Fossil Fuels Unused When Limiting Global Warming to 2 °C." *Nature* 517 (7533): 187–90.

9. Stevens, Paul, Glada Lahn, and Jaakko Kooroshy. 2015. "The Resource Curse Revisited." Chatham House Research Paper, London.

10. van der Ploeg, Frederick, and Cees Withagen. 2015. "Global Warming and the Green Paradox: A Review of Adverse Effects of Climate Policies." *Review of Environmental Economics and Policy* 9 (2): 285–303.

11. Venables, Anthony J. 2016. "Using Natural Resources for Development: Why Has It Proven So Difficult?" *Journal of Economic Perspectives* 30 (1): 161–84.

The Fossil Fuel Industry and Human Rights Violations

Common Dreams

Common Dreams is a progressive news organization dedicated to informing the public and inspiring change.

The fossil fuel industry largely behind the global climate crisis is contributing to the violation of a number of human rights, aggravating the conditions of persons, groups, and peoples in already vulnerable situations across the planet, warns a report by 350.org.

Oil, gas and coal companies are directly or indirectly responsible for some of the worst human rights abuses committed by corporations around the world in the last three decades. Two cases from Africa stand out from the report: Shell in Ogoniland (Nigeria) and Amu Power in Lamu (Kenya).

In Nigeria, the impacts associated with Shell's operations in the Niger Delta are perhaps the most notorious case of human rights abuses carried out by a fossil fuel corporation worldwide, sometimes with the complicity and direct involvement of state authorities. An estimated nine to thirteen million barrels of crude oil has reportedly been spilt in the Niger Delta since the commencement of commercial oil exploration and production in 1958. Protests against widespread and persistent oil pollution have been brutally repressed, with loss of life and a series of other egregious human rights violations. Victims of severe human rights abuses associated with oil extraction in the Niger Delta are still awaiting remediation of the harm caused to their lands, water and livelihood, in spite of multiple victories before courts and human rights bodies.

"As Fossil Fuel Companies Keep Driving the Climate Crisis, the Scale of Human Rights Violations Is Increasing, Alerts 350.org Report," Common Dreams, February 7, 2020. Licensed under CC BY-4.0 International..

In 2013, the Kenyan government set forth a proposal to build East Africa's first coal power plant in the proximity of Lamu Old Town, a UNESCO world heritage site on the Kenyan coast. Community groups have protested against plans to develop the plant, citing that its construction is unnecessary, as Kenya has sufficient renewable energy resources. Protesters against the plant have been harassed, two activists disappeared, with one presumed dead. However, in June 2019, a tribunal upheld the decision to revoke the licence given to Amu Power—one of the project financiers—on the grounds that an Environmental Impact Assessment (EIA) had not been properly conducted. The tribunal ordered Amu Power to undertake a new EIA if it wants to continue with construction, effectively halting any further work.

Landry Ninteretse, the Africa Managing Director of 350.org said, "Countries where these violations are being committed, have to enforce measures protecting communities affected by the human rights abuses caused by fossil fuel companies. Most of them have signed international treaties obliging them to protect threatened individuals, guarantee the right to protest and respect the decisions of Indigenous communities. Such mechanisms have to be enforced, legitimized and respected. The failure to do so represents a violation of States human right obligations."

According to this report, considering just a few major cases of violations, the fossil fuel industry was directly responsible for about 45,000 premature deaths caused by health issues, the dump of more than 18 billion gallons of toxic wastewater into rivers and the opening of almost 2.5 million acres of previously inaccessible indigenous homeland to land speculation, colonisation and deforestation.

With the aggravation of the climate crisis, the negative environmental and social impacts of the actions of fossil fuel companies in several of these cases—and similar ones—are getting worse. The pollution and contamination often caused by fossil fuel industry activities mainly affect the poorest populations, as well as the climate crisis. Vulnerable communities are being doubly exposed to losses or scarcity of land, fish stocks and water.

The 350.org report also highlights the need for local and national governments to act to protect climate defenders, such as community leaders who are at the forefront of mobilizations for the rights of affected families. Many of them are targets of threats, aggression, torture or murder.

An exemplary case mentioned by the report is the one of Ken Saro Wiwa, a well known environmental and human rights activist and minority spokesperson. His resistance to the fossil fuel companies as well as speaking against the exploitation of the Ogoni people, a minority group, saw Ken Saro Wiwa and eight other people executed by hanging on November 10, 1995, leaving the whole of Nigeria and the world in total shock.

Climate Change Is a Human Rights Problem

Amnesty International

Amnesty International is a nongovernmental organization dedicated to solving human rights problems.

"It's abundantly clear that climate change is already having an impact on human rights. And that this impact will only intensify in coming years."

> —*Kumi Naidoo,*
> *Secretary General of*
> *Amnesty International*

Millions of people are already suffering from the catastrophic effects of extreme disasters exacerbated by climate change—from prolonged drought in sub-Saharan Africa to devastating tropical storms sweeping across Southeast Asia, the Caribbean and the Pacific. During the summer months for the northern hemisphere in 2018, communities from the Arctic Circle to Greece, Japan, Pakistan and the USA experienced devastating heatwaves and wildfires that resulted in the deaths of hundreds of people.

While we largely understand climate change through the impacts it will have on our natural world, it is the devastation that it is causing and will continue to cause for humanity that makes it an urgent human rights issue. It will compound and magnify existing inequalities. And its effects will continue to grow and worsen over time, creating ruin for current and future generations.

This is why the failure of governments to act on climate change in the face of overwhelming scientific evidence may well be the biggest inter-generational human rights violation in history.

What Is Climate Change?

The planet's climate has constantly been changing over geological time, with significant fluctuations of global average temperatures.

However, this current period of warming is occurring more rapidly than any past events. It has become clear that humanity has caused most of the last century's warming by releasing heat-trapping gases—commonly referred to as greenhouse gases—to power our modern lives. We are doing this through burning fossil fuels, agriculture and land-use and other activities that drive climate change. Greenhouse gases are at the highest levels they have ever been over the last 800,000 years. This rapid rise is a problem because it's changing our climate at a rate that is too fast for living things to adapt to.

Climate change involves not only rising temperatures, but also extreme weather events, rising sea levels, shifting wildlife populations and habitats, and a range of other impacts.

What Causes Climate Change?

> We are humans who want the same thing every other human wants—a safe place to live on this planet we call home. So while our work must continue to be unbiased and objective, increasingly we are raising our voices, adding to the clear message that climate change is real and humans are responsible, the impacts are serious and we must act now.
>
> —Katharine Hayhoe, Climate Scientist

There is an overwhelming scientific consensus that global warming is mostly man-made: 97% of climate scientists have come to this conclusion.

One of the biggest drivers by far is our burning of fossil fuels—coal, gas and oil—which has increased the concentration of greenhouse gases—such as carbon dioxide—in our atmosphere.

This, coupled with other activities like clearing land for agriculture, is causing the average temperature of our planet to increase. In fact, scientists are as certain of the link between greenhouse gases and global warming as they are of the link between smoking and lung cancer.

This is not a recent conclusion. The scientific community has collected and studied the data on this for decades. Warnings about global warming started making headlines back in the late 1980s.

In 1992, 165 nations signed an international treaty, the UN Framework Convention on Climate Change (UNFCCC). They have held meetings annually ever since (called "Conference of the Parties" or COP), with the aim of developing goals and methods to reduce climate change as well as adapt to its already visible effects. Today, 197 countries are bound by the UNFCCC.

What Are the Effects of Climate Change?

> The Wilmington community, they are mostly low income, so the heat waves are very detrimental because they cannot afford air-conditioning. And because they are still close to the refineries and to oil extraction, they have to shut their windows.
>
> —Alicia Rivera, Community Organizer and Climate Activist,
> USA

The effects of climate change are already being felt now, but they will get worse. Global warming has reached approximately 1°C above pre-industrial levels. Every half degree (or even less) of global warming counts.

It is important to remember that no one list of the effects of climate change can be exhaustive. It is very likely that heatwaves will occur more often and last longer, and that extreme precipitation events will become more intense and frequent in many regions. The oceans will continue to warm and acidify, and global mean sea level will continue to rise. All of this will have, and is already starting to have, a devastating impact on human life.

The urgent need to address climate change has become even clearer with the release of a major report in October 2018 by the world's leading scientific body for the assessment of climate change, the Intergovernmental Panel on Climate Change (IPCC). The IPCC warns that in order to avoid catastrophic global warming, we must not reach 1.5°C above pre-industrial levels—or at very minimum not exceed that. The report sets out the massive differences between the 1.5°C and 2°C scenarios.

By working to limit the increase in average global average temperatures to 1.5°C, the IPCC states that we could for example:

- reduce the number of people both exposed to climate-related risks and susceptible to poverty by up to several hundred million by 2050;
- protect 10 million people from risks related to sea levels;
- reduce the proportion of the global population exposed to increase in water stress by up to 50%, or one in every 25 people on this planet.

Perhaps most importantly, the IPCC report gave the world a clear deadline to avoid catastrophe: greenhouse gas emissions must be halved from their 2010 levels by 2030 to avoid reaching 1.5°C. Our governments must therefore take immediate steps right now to change course. The longer we take to do this, the more we will have to rely on costly technologies that could have harmful impacts on human rights.

UN Secretary-General Antonio Guterres told states that they must set credible targets by 2020 to stop the increase of emissions, otherwise "we risk missing the point where we can avoid runaway climate change, with disastrous consequences for people and all the natural systems that sustain us."

Who Is Impacted the Most by Climate Change?

You say you love your children above all else, and yet you are stealing their future in front of their very eyes.

—Greta Thunberg, Climate Activist and Founder of Climate
School Strike

Climate change is and will continue to harm all of us unless governments take action. However, its effects are likely to be much more pronounced for certain groups—for example, those communities dependent on agricultural or coastal livelihoods—as well as those who are generally already vulnerable, disadvantaged and subject to discrimination.

These are some of the ways climate change can and is exacerbating inequalities:

Between Developed and Developing Nations
At a national level, those in low-lying, small island states and less developed countries will be and already are among those worst affected. People in the Marshall Islands already regularly experience the devastating flooding and storms that destroy their homes and livelihoods. The 2018 heatwave in the northern hemisphere made headlines across Europe and North America, but some of the worst effects were also felt in places like Pakistan, where more than 60 people died—mostly labourers already working in intense heat—as temperatures soared above 44°C.

Between Different Ethnicities and Classes
The effects of climate change and fossil fuel-related pollution also run along ethnicity and class lines. In North America, it is largely poorer communities of colour who are forced to breathe toxic air because their neighbourhoods are more likely to be situated next to power plants and refineries. They experience markedly higher rates of respiratory illnesses and cancers, and African Americans are three times more likely to die of airborne pollution than the overall US population.

Between Genders
Women and girls are disproportionately affected by climate change, reflecting the fact that they are more likely in many countries to be marginalized and disadvantaged. This means that they are more vulnerable to the impacts of climate-related events as they

are less able to protect themselves against it and will find it harder to recover.

Between Generations
Future generations will experience the worsening effects unless action is taken now by governments. However, children and young people are already suffering due to their specific metabolism, physiology and developmental needs. This means, for example, that the forced displacement experienced by communities impacting a whole range of rights—from water, sanitation and food to adequate housing, health, education and development—is likely to be particularly harmful to children.

Between Communities
Indigenous peoples are among the communities most impacted by climate change. They often live in marginal lands and fragile ecosystems which are particularly sensitive to alterations in the physical environment. They maintain a close connection with nature and their traditional lands on which their livelihoods and cultural identity depend.

Why Is Climate Change a Human Rights Issue?

Climate change is a human rights issue not only because its devastating impacts affect the enjoyment of human rights, but also because it is a man-made phenomenon which can be mitigated by governments.

—Kumi Naidoo, Secretary General of Amnesty International

Human rights are intimately linked with climate change because of its devastating effect on not just the environment but our own wellbeing. In addition to threatening our very existence, climate change is having harmful impacts on our rights to life, health, food, water, housing and livelihoods.

The longer governments wait to take meaningful action, the harder the problem becomes to solve, and the greater the risk that emissions will be reduced through means that increase inequality rather than reduce it.

These are some of the ways climate change is impacting and will impact our human rights:

Right to Life

We all have the right to life, and to live in freedom and safety. But climate change threatens the safety of billions of people on this planet. The most obvious example is through extreme weather-related events, such as storms, floods and wildfires. Typhoon Yolanda in the Philippines claimed the lives of nearly 10,000 people in 2013. Heat stress is among the most deadly impacts. The summer heatwave in Europe in 2003 resulted in the deaths of 35,000 people. However, there are many other less visible ways that climate change threatens lives. The World Health Organization predicts that climate change will cause 250,000 deaths per year between 2030 and 2050, due to malaria, malnutrition, diarrhoea and heat stress.

Right to Health

We all have the right to enjoy the highest attainable standard of physical and mental health. According to the IPCC, the major health impacts of climate change will include greater risk of injury, disease and death due to more intense heatwaves and fires; increased risk of under-nutrition as a result of diminished food production in poor regions; and increased risks of food- and water-borne diseases, and vector-borne diseases. Children exposed to traumatic events such as natural disasters, exacerbated by climate change, can suffer from post-traumatic stress disorders. The health impacts of climate change demand an urgent response, with unmitigated warming threatening to undermine health systems and core global health objectives.

Right to Housing

We all have a right to an adequate standard of living for ourselves and our families, including adequate housing. However, climate change threatens our right to housing in a variety of ways. Extreme weather events like floods and wildfires are already destroying people's homes, leaving them displaced. Drought, erosion and flooding can also over time change the environment whilst sea-level rises threaten the homes of millions of people around the world in low-lying territories.

Rights to Water and to Sanitation

We all have the right to safe water for personal and domestic use and to sanitation that ensures we stay healthy. But a combination of factors such as melting snow and ice, reduced rainfall, higher temperatures and rising sea levels show that climate change is affecting and will continue to affect the quality and quantity of water resources. Already more than one billion people do not have access to clean water, and climate change will make this worse. Extreme weather events such as cyclones and floods affect water and sanitation infrastructure, leaving behind contaminated water and thus contributing to the spread of water-borne diseases. Sewage systems, especially in urban areas, will also be affected.

Who Is Responsible for Stopping Climate Change?

After placing plantiffs in a position of climate danger, defendants have continued to act with deliberate indifference to the known danger they helped create and enhance. A destabilized climate system poses unusually serious risks of harm to plaintiff's lives and their bodily integrity and dignity.

—*Juliana vs United States Government*, Lawsuit Filed by Children Against the US Government

States

States have the obligation to mitigate the harmful effects of climate change by taking the most ambitious measures possible to prevent or reduce greenhouse emissions within the shortest possible time-frame. While wealthy states need to lead the way, both internally and through international cooperation, all countries must take all reasonable steps to reduce emissions to the full extent of their abilities.

States must also take all necessary steps to help everyone within their jurisdiction to adapt to the foreseeable and unavoidable effects of climate change, thus minimizing the impact of climate change on their human rights. This is true irrespective of whether the state is responsible for those effects, because states have an obligation to protect people from harms caused by third parties.

States must take steps to tackle climate change as fast and as humanely as possible. In their efforts to address climate change, they must not resort to measures that directly or indirectly violate human rights. For example, conservation areas or renewable energy projects must not be created on the lands of Indigenous peoples without consulting them and getting their consent.

In all measures, states should respect the right to information and participation for all affected people, as well as their right to access effective remedies for human rights abuses.

However, the current pledges made by governments to mitigate climate change are completely inadequate, as they would lead to a catastrophic 3°C increase in average global temperatures over pre-industrial levels by 2100. People in countries including France, the Netherlands and Switzerland are taking their governments to court for their failure to establish sufficient climate mitigation targets and measures.

Corporations

Businesses also have a responsibility to respect human rights. To meet this responsibility, companies must assess the potential effects of their activities on human rights and put in place measures to prevent negative impacts. They must make such findings and any prevention measures public. Companies must also take measures to remedy human rights abuses they cause or to which they contribute, either by themselves or in cooperation with other actors. Such responsibilities extend to human rights harms resulting from climate change.

Corporations, and particularly fossil fuel companies, must also immediately put measures in place to minimize greenhouse emissions—including by shifting their portfolio towards renewable energy—and make relevant information about their emissions and mitigation efforts public. These efforts must extend to all the major subsidiaries, affiliates and entities in their supply chain.

Fossil fuel companies have been historically among the most responsible for climate change—and this continues today. Research shows that just 100 fossil fuel-producing companies are responsible for 71% of global greenhouse gas emissions since 1988.

There is growing evidence that major fossil fuel companies have known for decades about the harmful effects of burning fossil fuels and have attempted to suppress that information and block efforts to tackle climate change.

Why Do We Need to Stop Climate Change?

Because we all deserve equal protection. We are all born with fundamental human rights, yet these rights are under grave threat from climate change. While climate change threatens all of our lives in some way or other, people who experience discrimination are among those likely to be the worst affected. We are all equally deserving of protection from this universal threat.

Because there is nothing to lose from acting, and everything to gain. Fighting climate change gives us a chance to put the wellbeing of people first by ensuring a right to a healthy environment. This will give us an opportunity to enhance human rights, for example by enabling more people to access cleaner and cheaper energy resources and create job opportunities in new sectors.

Because we have the knowledge, power and ability to stop climate change. Many people are already working on creative, inspiring and innovative solutions to address climate change. From citizens to companies to cities, there are people all over the world actively working on policies and campaigns and solutions that will protect people and the planet. Indigenous peoples and minority communities have for centuries developed sustainable ways of living with the environments that they call home. We can learn from them and, with their consent, benefit from their know-how to inform our own efforts to find a different way of interacting with our planet.

What Is Amnesty Doing to Address Climate Change?

There is an urgent need to put people and human rights at the centre of the climate change conversation. For Amnesty International and other human rights organizations, this means pushing for accountability for states who fail to act on climate change, just as we do with other human rights violations.

—Chiara Liguori, Policy Adviser, Amnesty International

Amnesty International's work on climate change has included standing up for human rights in the Paris Agreement on climate change, contributing to stronger human rights standards on climate change, and supporting environmental groups as they put forward human rights arguments.

Given the urgency of this issue, we will deepen our involvement by playing a galvanizing role for the human rights community as it shows how climate change is impacting people's rights and how people are responding to the reality and the threat of climate change.

Amnesty will work with a variety of different groups in key countries to mount pressure against governments and corporations which are obstructing progress. Amnesty will support young people, but also Indigenous peoples, trade unions and affected communities, to demand a rapid and just transition to a zero-carbon economy that leaves no one behind. Litigation and the use of national and regional human rights mechanisms will be additional tools to keep up the pressure.

Amnesty International will build on its work in support of environmental defenders to specifically facilitate the work of those protecting land, food, communities and people against climate impacts, extraction and expansion of fossil fuels and deforestation. Defending the civic space for information, participation and mobilization will also contribute towards promoting more progressive climate policies.

Our Demands

Amnesty is calling for governments to:

- Do everything they can to help stop the global temperature rising by more than 1.5°C.
- Reduce their greenhouse gas emissions to zero by 2050 at the latest. Richer countries should do this faster. By 2030, global emissions must be half as much as they were in 2010.
- Stop using fossil fuels (coal, oil and gas) as quickly as possible.
- Make sure that climate action is done in a way that does not violate anyone's human rights, and reduces rather than increases inequality.
- Make sure everyone, in particularly those affected by climate change or the transition to a fossil-free economy, is properly informed about what is happening and is able to participate in decisions about their futures.
- Work together to fairly share the burden of climate change— richer countries must help others.

Transitioning to the Green Economy Would Create Jobs

International Labour Organization

The International Labour Organization is a United Nations agency tasked with creating policy to protect workers.

The transformation to a greener economy could generate 15 to 60 million additional jobs globally over the next two decades and lift tens of millions of workers out of poverty, according to a new report led by the Green Jobs Initiative.

The study "Working towards sustainable development: Opportunities for decent work and social inclusion in a green economy" says that these gains will depend on whether the right set of policies are put in place.

"The current development model has proven to be inefficient and unsustainable, not only for the environment, but for economies and societies as well," said ILO Director-General Juan Somavia. "We urgently need to move to a sustainable development path with a coherent set of policies with people and the planet at the centre."

"The forthcoming 'Rio+20' United Nations conference will be a crucial moment to make sure decent work and social inclusion are integral parts of any future development strategy," he added.

Achim Steiner, Executive Director of the UN Environment Programme (UNEP), said: "This report comes on the eve of World Environment Day on 5 June under the theme Green Economy: Does It Include You?"

"The findings underline that it can include millions more people in terms of overcoming poverty and delivering improved livelihoods for this and future generations. It is a positive message of opportunity in a troubled world of challenges that we are relaying

"Transition to Green Economy Could Yield up to 60 Million Jobs, ILO Says," International Labour Organization, May 31, 2012. Reprinted by permission.

to capital cities across the globe as leaders prepare and plan for the Rio+20 Summit," he added.

The report—published almost four years after the first study by the Green Jobs Initiative—looks at the impact that the greening of the economy can have on employment, incomes and sustainable development in general.

At least half of the global workforce—the equivalent of 1.5 billion people—will be affected by the transition to a greener economy. While changes will be felt throughout the economy, eight key sectors are expected to play a central role and be mostly affected: agriculture, forestry, fishing, energy, resource-intensive manufacturing, recycling, building and transport.

Tens of millions of jobs have already been created by this transformation. For example the renewable energy sector now employs close to 5 million workers, more than doubling the number of jobs from 2006-2010. Energy efficiency is another important source of green jobs, particularly in the construction industry, the sector hardest hit by the economic crisis.

In the United States, three million people are employed in environmental goods and services. In Spain, there are now more than half a million jobs in this sector.

Net gains in employment in the order of 0.5–2 per cent of total employment are possible. In emerging economies and developing countries, the gains are likely to be higher than in industrialized countries, because the former can leapfrog to green technology rather than replace obsolete resource-intensive infrastructure. Brazil has already created just under three million jobs, accounting for some 7 per cent of all formal employment.

No Gains Without the Right Policies

These good results have one thing in common: the recognition that environmental and socio-economic challenges need to be addressed in a comprehensive and complementary manner.

- First, this means promoting and implementing sustainable production processes at the level of the business itself, especially among small-and-medium-sized enterprises in the key sectors mentioned above.

- Second, an extension of social protection, income support and skills training measures is key to ensuring that workers are in a position to take advantage of these new opportunities.
- Third, international labour standards and workers' rights can provide a legal and institutional framework, as well as practical guidance, for work in a greener and sustainable economy, especially when it comes to job quality and occupational safety and health.
- Finally, effective social dialogue involving employers and trade unions is central to the governance of sustainable development.

"Environmental sustainability is not a job killer, as it is sometimes claimed. On the contrary, if properly managed, it can lead to more and better jobs, poverty reduction and social inclusion," said the ILO head.

Other Key Findings of the Report

- In the EU alone, 14.6 million direct and indirect jobs exist in the protection of biodiversity and rehabilitation of natural resources and forests.
- The targeted international investments of US$30 billion/ year into reduced deforestation and degradation of forests could sustain up to 8 million additional full-time workers in developing countries.
- Experiences from Colombia, Brazil and other countries show that the formalization and organisation of some 15-20 million informal waste pickers could have significant economic, social and environmental benefits.
- The building renovation programme for energy efficiency in Germany is an example of the possible win-win-win outcomes: it has mobilized €100 billion in investments; it

is reducing energy bills, avoiding emissions and creating around 300,000 direct jobs per year.

- Overuse of natural resources has already caused large losses, including over a million jobs for forest workers, mainly in Asia, because of unsustainable forest management practices.
- The fisheries sector is likely to face a major, albeit temporary transition challenge for workers due to overfishing. Temporary reductions of catch may be needed in many fisheries to allow declining stocks to recover. Of particular concern is that 95 per cent of the 45 million workers employed in fishing are often poor artisanal coastal fishermen in developing countries.
- In much of Asia, Africa, Latin America and parts of Europe, the proportion of expenditure on energy by poor households is three times—and can be as much as 20 times—that of richer households.
- The National Rural Employment Guarantee Act in India and the social housing and "green grants" programmes in Brazil are good examples of social protection policies that contribute to sustainable development.
- Women could be among the main beneficiaries of a greener, more socially inclusive economy, with better access to opportunities to jobs, for example in renewable energy, higher incomes, in particular in agriculture, formalization of employment, notably among the 15–20 million recycling workers and many burdens reduced among other from access to clean energy, enhanced food security, energy and water efficient social housing.
- A mere 8–12 per cent of the workforce in industrialized countries, for example, is employed in the 10–15 industries generating 70–80 per cent of CO_2 emissions. Only a fraction of these is likely to lose their jobs if policies are adopted to green existing enterprises and to promote employment.

The Green Economy Is About More Than the Environment

Green Economy Coalition

The Green Economy Coalition is an organization that works to advance the green economy and that helps connect actors invested in that transition.

Humanity faces serious challenges in the coming decades: climate change, biodiversity loss, growing inequality, and more. These systemic global crises cannot be tackled in isolation, because they are all interconnected. But our economic systems are not fit enough to deliver a good balance of environmental and social goals.

Economies are, at heart, a collection of rules and norms that reward some behaviours and punish others. In their current form, our economies incentivise overconsumption, degrade communal bonds, and destroy natural wealth. But this is not inevitable or unavoidable; it is simply how our economies have evolved to operate. To solve these problems, a new economic vision is required.

The Vision: A Fair, Green Economic Future

Our vision of a green economy is one that provides prosperity for all within the ecological limits of the planet. It follows five key principles, each of which draws on important precedents in international policy, and which together can guide economic reform in diverse contexts.

1. The Wellbeing Principle

A green economy enables all people to create and enjoy prosperity.

- The green economy is people-centred. Its purpose is to create genuine, shared prosperity.
- It focuses on growing wealth that will support wellbeing. This wealth is not merely financial, but includes the full range of human, social, physical and natural capitals.
- It prioritizes investment and access to the sustainable natural systems, infrastructure, knowledge and education needed for all people to prosper.
- It offers opportunities for green and decent livelihoods, enterprises and jobs.
- It is built on collective action for public goods, yet is based on individual choices

2. The Justice Principle

The green economy promotes equity within and between generations.

- The green economy is inclusive and non-discriminatory. It shares decision-making, benefits and costs fairly; avoids elite capture; and especially supports women's empowerment.
- It promotes the equitable distribution of opportunity and outcome, reducing disparities between people, while also giving sufficient space for wildlife and wilderness.
- It takes a long-term perspective on the economy, creating wealth and resilience that serve the interests of future citizens, while also acting urgently to tackle today's multi-dimensional poverty and injustice.
- It is based on solidarity and social justice, strengthening trust and social ties, and supporting human rights, the rights of workers, indigenous peoples and minorities, and the right to sustainable development.
- It promotes empowerment of MSMEs, social enterprises, and sustainable livelihoods.
- It seeks a fast and fair transition and covers its costs—leaving no-one behind, enabling vulnerable groups to be agents of transition, and innovating in social protection and reskilling.

3. The Planetary Boundaries Principle

The green economy safeguards, restores and invests in nature.

- An inclusive green economy recognizes and nurtures nature's diverse values—functional values of providing goods and services that underpin the economy, nature's cultural values that underpin societies, and nature's ecological values that underpin all of life itself.
- It acknowledges the limited substitutability of natural capital with other capitals, employing the precautionary principle to avoid loss of critical natural capital and breaching ecological limits.
- It invests in protecting, growing and restoring biodiversity, soil, water, air, and natural systems.
- It is innovative in managing natural systems, informed by their properties such as circularity, and aligning with local community livelihoods based on biodiversity and natural systems.

4. The Efficiency and Sufficiency Principle

The green economy is geared to support sustainable consumption as well as sustainable production.

- An inclusive green economy is low-carbon, resource-conserving, diverse and circular. It embraces new models of economic development that address the challenge of creating prosperity within planetary boundaries.
- It recognises there must be a significant global shift to limit consumption of natural resources to physically sustainable levels if we are to remain within planetary boundaries.
- It recognizes a "social floor" of basic goods and services consumption that is essential to meet people's wellbeing and dignity, as well as unacceptable "peaks" of consumption.
- It aligns prices, subsidies and incentives with true costs to society, through mechanisms where the "polluter pays"

and/or where benefits accrue to those who deliver inclusive green outcomes.

5. The Good Governance Principle

The green economy is guided by integrated, accountable and resilient institutions.

- An inclusive green economy is evidence-based—its norms and institutions are interdisciplinary, deploying both sound science and economics along with local knowledge for adaptive strategy.
- It is supported by institutions that are integrated, collaborative and coherent—horizontally across sectors and vertically across governance levels—and with adequate capacity to meet their respective roles in effective, efficient and accountable ways.
- It requires public participation, prior informed consent, transparency, social dialogue, democratic accountability, and freedom from vested interests in all institutions—public, private and civil society—so that enlightened leadership is complemented by societal demand.
- It promotes devolved decision-making for local economies and management of natural systems while maintaining strong common, centralized standards, procedures, and compliance systems.
- It builds a financial system with the purpose of delivering wellbeing and sustainability, set up in ways that safely serve the interests of society.

The green economy is a universal and transformative change to the global status quo. It will require a fundamental shift in government priorities. Realising this change is not easy, but it is necessary if we are ever to achieve the Sustainable Development Goals.

Green Growth May Hurt, Not Help, the Poor

Linda Kleemann, Kacana Sipangule, and Pablo Selaya

Linda Kleemann and Kacana Sipangule are both researchers at the Kiel Institute for World Economy. Pablo Selaya is an economics professor at the University of Copenhagen and visiting scholar at Harvard University.

The terms "green growth and green economy" stand for reconciling business activities and expanding economies with nature. They have been on the agenda of policymakers as well as researchers in recent years, inspiring international debate in a time of financial crises and recession. The guiding idea is to fulfil the principle of sustainable development, which was accepted by the international community at the Earth Summit in Rio de Janeiro in 1992 and reaffirmed at the stock-taking conference Rio+20 last year. The goal is to eliminate poverty and to respect our planet's environmental boundaries at the same time.

In the run-up to Rio+20, several developing countries embraced green strategies for economic development, and many others at least considered doing so. Costa Rica, Sri Lanka, Mauritius, Ghana and Bangladesh are among the many developing nations that take formal account of environmental matters in their national development plans. Rwanda and Ethiopia are considered African beacons, because they have incorporated aspects of green economy into their national growth strategies.

The desire for more environmentally sustainable policies in the developing world is reflected in the Bamako Declaration of African ministers at an AU conference in 2010 (quoted in UNEP 2011): "We will pay our part to spearhead the transition to a green economy in Africa (…) to ensure that green economies contribute

"Shades of Green," by Linda Kleemann, Kacana Sipangule, and Pablo Selaya, D+C Development and Cooperation, June 18, 2013. Reprinted by permission.

to sustainable development and poverty reduction objectives." Other global leaders have expressed similar optimism. But here are sceptics too. Some experts doubt that green growth can do much to reduce poverty. The core question is whether environmentally-friendly policies are beneficial or detrimental for the poor?

To answer this question one must first identify who the poor are, where they live, and how green-growth strategies will impact on their livelihoods. Extensive work by Andy Sumner (2012, 2012b) shows that the majority of the world's poor no longer live in low-income countries, but instead in middle-income countries. The implications of green policies, however, are different in low-income and middle-income countries.

Most studies published by international organisations and donor agencies indicate considerable advantages of green-growth strategies for low-income countries. The UN Environment Programme (UNEP 2011) argues, for instance, that many least-developed countries (LDCs) stand to benefit. The essential reason is that their natural capital matters very much in economic activity and must not be compromised by environmentally destructive industries. Moreover, renewable energy solutions offer convincing options for rural electrification, which will contribute to raising people from misery. At the same time, the growth of the renewables sector will generate local jobs.

In line with such assessments, Ethiopia's current Climate-Resilient Green-Economy Strategy aims to achieve the status of a middle-income country through renewable technologies and energy efficiency. Among other things, the strategy tackles issues such as rural electrification, improved agricultural productivity and forest protection. Feasibility will certainly depend on international policies on climate finance and carbon credits, but there can be no doubt that the strategy has a huge potential.

Ambiguous Perspective

For middle-income countries and emerging markets things look different. Many of them experienced high growth rates based on carbon-intensive development in recent years. Much of their existing infrastructure is based on the use of fossil fuels. Accordingly, the transformation to a green economy will be costly in political and economic terms. Deteriorating environmental conditions will adversely affect many poor people of course, but so will rising costs for the energy-related services they rely on.

Green-growth strategies are therefore more ambiguous from poor people's views in middle-income countries than in low-income countries. In regard to poverty, Holle Wlokas et al. (2012) argue that middle-income countries are better advised to focus on the mitigation of climate change rather than climate protection. Their assessment is based on several case studies.

Scholars and non-governmental organisations warn against adopting green-growth strategies in haste, without first analysing the implications diligently. There may indeed be considerable trade-offs between environmental sustainability and poverty reduction even in low-income countries. Danielle Resnick et al. (2012) have shown that green-growth policies can encourage countries like Malawi to redesign strategies in ways that may be inconsistent with their comparative advantages and current development pathways.

Resnick et al. refer to Malawi's successful Agricultural Input Subsidy Programme (AISP), which has made a dent in rural poverty and significantly improved food security. The downside is that AISP leads to more greenhouse-gas emissions because it depends on chemical fertilisers. Malawi's government must thus choose between a strategy that has proven successful and others that are more sustainable in the long run but do less to reduce poverty in the short run. Organic fertilisers are a viable alternative and so are intercropping and minimum tillage. However, these practices are not common in Malawi.

In contrast to many reports that point out that the poor will benefit from green policies, Stefan Dercon (2012) argues in rather general terms that the poor are likely to suffer. According to conventional development theory, economic growth results from a structural transformation in which agriculture becomes less important as other sectors that yield higher returns thrive. Dercon emphasises, however, that the new industries must be labour intensive for poor people to benefit from that transformation. He warns that green-growth policies will not improve poor people's livelihoods because they will fail to absorb surplus labour from rural areas if they rely on capital-intensive technologies and high-skill employment.

Research of this kind indicates that green growth is certainly not a panacea. Policy implications must be assessed carefully in every single case. It makes sense to consider varying shades of green and let countries tailor their own strategies according to their specific needs.

The Way Forward

Evidently, there is a need for more research on the matter. We need a better understanding of the local impacts of green-growth strategies, and must assess the trade-offs between short-term and long-term effects. Most of the current literature is based on stylized facts, so more empirical evidence is required to design good policies for developing countries.

This year's annual PEGNet conference will focus on these questions in Copenhagen on 17 and 18 October. PEGNet is a network that links research institutions, policymakers and development agencies at an international level. Its sponsors include Germany's Federal Ministry for Economic Cooperation and Development, the agencies GIZ and KFW as well as the Kiel Institute for the World Economy and Göttingen University. This year's event will be hosted in cooperation with the Department of Economics at the University of Copenhagen. An innovative addition will be a "speedmatching session" that will put non-governmental organisations in touch with development researchers, government agencies and policy makers.

References

1. Dercon, S., 2012: Is green growth good for the poor? World Bank Policy Research Working Paper 6231. http://elibrary.worldbank.org/content /workingpaper/10.1596/1813-9450-6231

2. Resnick, D., Tarp, F., and Thurlow, J., 2012: The political economy of green growth: illustrations from Southern Africa. UNU-WIDER Working Paper No. 2012/11. http://www.wider.unu.edu/stc/repec/pdfs/wp2012/wp2012-011.pdf

3. Sumner, A., 2012: Where will the world's poor live? IDS, University of Sussex: http://www.ids.ac.uk/publication/where-will-the-world-s-poor-live-global -poverty-projections-for-2020-and-2030

4. Sumner, A., 2012b: The new face of poverty: how has the composition of poverty in low-income and lower middle-income countries changed since the 1990s? IDS Working Paper 408/2012. http://onlinelibrary.wiley.com/doi/10.1111/j.2040 -0209.2012.00408.x/abstract

5. UNEP, 2011: Green economy: why a green economy matters for the least-developed countries. A joint publication of UNEP with UNCTAD and UN_ OHRLLS. http://www.un-ngls.org/spip.php?article3400

6. Wlokas, H., Rennkamp, B., Torres, M., Winkler, H., et al., 2012: MAPS—Low carbon development and poverty—Exploring poverty-alleviating mitigation action in developing countries. Univ. of Cape Town. http://www.erc.uct.ac.za /Staff/Wlokas.htm

Saudi Arabia Has Long Stood in the Way of Climate Progress

Lee Fang and Sharon Lerner

Lee Fang is a journalist and cofounder of Republic Report, a blog that covers political corruption that syndicates content with prestigious media outlets. Sharon Lerner is an investigative reporter for the Intercept, covering health and the environment.

Anyone who was still questioning whether climate change can exacerbate violent international conflicts has only to look at Saudi Arabia, where drones struck oil installations in the eastern part of the country on September 14. While the Trump administration is blaming Iran, Houthis in Yemen claimed responsibility for the attack on Saudi Aramco, the state-owned oil company, which is both the source of the kingdom's vast wealth and, as the world's largest corporate emitter of greenhouse gases, one of the primary drivers of the climate emergency making life increasingly difficult throughout the region.

Rising temperatures have exacerbated water shortages in Yemen, where some 19 million people already lacked access to clean water and sanitation due to mismanagement and drought. Saudis have weaponized this water scarcity in their war in Yemen, targeting areas for their proximity to fertile land and destroying water infrastructure.

Meanwhile, Saudi Arabia is also facing some of the worst risks from soaring temperatures. This summer, the temperature in Al Majmaah, a city in central Saudi Arabia, reached 131 degrees Fahrenheit, while rapid desertification was reported throughout the Arabian peninsula.

"Saudi Arabia Denies Its Key Role in Climate Change Even As It Prepares for the Worst," by Lee Fang and Sharon Lerner. Originally published on September 18, 2019. Republished with permission from The Intercept, an award-winning nonprofit news organization dedicated to holding the powerful accountable through fearless, adversarial journalism. https://theintercept.com/2019/09/18/saudi-arabia-aramco-oil-climate-change/.

Saudi Aramco, the most profitable corporation in the world, released more than 40 billion metric tons of greenhouse gases between 1992 and 2017, the equivalent of almost 5 percent of industrial carbon dioxide and methane. The company, closely held by the Saudi royal family, is now confronting the challenges of climate change in ways that mirror many western fossil fuel giants: by launching a rebranding effort that positions the firm as an environmental leader.

"There is no limit to our industry's potential if we can meet society's demand for ultra-clean energy," said Amin Nasser, the chief executive of Aramco, at the World Energy Congress in Abu Dhabi, United Arab Emirates, last week. Nasser led Aramco to help found the Oil and Gas Climate Initiative, a splashy new effort to showcase the oil industry's pledge to achieve "global net zero emissions" in the spirit of meeting the "ambitions set by the Paris Agreement," the United Nations climate accord.

The company's various social media pages have driven home the argument. In one video, posted by Aramco last month and set to the wobbling bass beats of an EDM rave track, claims the Saudi oil giant has worked to leverage its research power "to deliver sizable reductions in CO2." Another promotional video touts the company's focus on emission control technology, stating that Aramco is "committed to urgent action on climate change."

But the Saudi oil company's lofty branding campaign belies a stunning history of undermining action to address the climate crisis, a concerted effort designed to preserve the profits of Aramco.

In stark contrast to its current splashy greenwashing campaign, Saudi Arabia has played a quiet yet powerful role in thwarting proactive climate policy at United Nations conferences and US domestic policy battles alike.

A History of Obstruction

For nearly thirty years, the Saudi delegation has played a deft role in obstructing global efforts to reduce carbon emissions.

"The Saudis have been very good in making sure only weak measures have been adopted," said Joanna Depledge, editor of the journal *Climate Policy*, who has written about Saudi obstructionism.

Since the Intergovernmental Panel on Climate Change meeting in Madrid, in 1995—when Mohammad Al-Sabban, then a Saudi petroleum official, famously confronted scientists, claiming the science around climate change was not settled—Saudi delegates have maneuvered to push for a series of delays.

Despite its vast oil wealth and high per capita income, Saudi Arabia often positioned itself as the voice of the developing world, winning the right to serve as a voice for the G-77 group of developing countries in climate talks. In this role, Saudi delegates have demanded steep concessions for poorer countries. The demands, while justified at face-value, have allowed Saudi negotiators to extract lengthy delays, at times while working in concert with Western oil interests.

Don Pearlman, a former lobbyist with the law firm now known as Squire Patton Boggs, once led the Global Climate Council, an ad-hoc lobby group of fossil fuel firms convened to prevent curbs on carbon pollution. Pearlman worked closely with the Saudi delegation to introduce a series of obstructionist motions to climate talks.

The US diplomatic cables released by Chelsea Manning further reveal Saudi intransigence on more recent climate negotiations. James Smith, then the US ambassador to Saudi Arabia, bemoaned the "obstructionism that Saudi negotiators have often shown," in an email relaying negotiation talks to State Department officials.

Al-Sabban, during the 2009 negotiations in Copenhagen for a climate accord, declared on television that "there is no relationship whatsoever between human activities and climate change," and added that, "whatever the international community does to reduce greenhouse gas emissions will have no effect on the climate's natural variability." Now retired from his government position, Al-Sabban hasn't changed his position. In recent tweets aimed at an American journalist, he declared, "Trump will be in the office for another term to kill all of your nonsense climate lies."

While Aramco has rebranded, the government strategy at impeding global climate negotiations has not.

While Saudi Arabia has been standing in the way of climate progress since the 1990s, "I almost wonder if it hasn't gotten worse," said Depledge, who noted that, during the most recent UN climate change negotiations in Katowice, Poland, "Saudi Arabia was picking at point after point" in the most recent report of the Intergovernmental Panel on Climate Change.

Saudi Arabia joined with the US, Russia, and Kuwait to object to wording welcoming that report, which was published last October and spelled out the impacts of warming 1.5 degrees Celsius above pre-industrial levels. The difference between 1.5 and 2 degrees of warming, which had been the focus of previous work, could expose an additional 10 million people to the threats of sea level rise and tens of millions of people to suffering from extreme heat, water scarcity, and flooding. The 0.5 degree difference is also expected to double the number of plant and animal species that will become extinct.

A Revealing Bond Sale

Saudi Arabia's posture in global climate talks belies its true position on the ramifications of global climate action.

Despite the glossy greenwashing spin in Aramco's latest publicity blitz, the company's true fears about a shift away from oil were revealed this year in its first-ever bond sale. The corporate debt, used to fund Aramco's acquisition of the Saudi Arabian plastics and chemical firm Sabic, included a corporate disclosure detailing the conditions that stand to endanger the profitability of the firm.

Aramco, the bond filing revealed, earns profits of over $111 billion a year. Future revenue, however, could be curtailed sharply if major economies begin transitioning to renewable energy.

"Climate change concerns and impacts could reduce global demand for hydrocarbons," the Aramco filing's risk section declares. The policies that could harm the demand for oil include "carbon emission cap and trade regimes, carbon taxes, increased energy efficiency standards and incentives and mandates for renewable energy."

Technological advances, such as electric vehicles, could also reduce the demand for refined oil products, the filing noted. Many governments around the world are moving to adopt carbon emission reductions in line with the Paris agreement, the Aramco filing further warns, a dynamic that could hasten reduction in the use of fossil fuels.

The filing also shows the company's focus on a range of petroleum products, including jet fuel. In the Katowice climate talks last year, Saudi Arabia, reflecting Aramco's interests in jet fuel production, objected to having the International Civil Aviation Organization report on the climate impacts of aviation.

Aramco did not respond to a request for comment.

Funding US Climate Denialism

Beyond the international stage, the influence of Saudi Arabia's lobbying clout has left an imprint on the domestic battles over climate change.

Saudi Arabia's lobbying prowess is legendary in Beltway circles, mostly for its influence over the lucrative sale of US arms and other hot-button issues. The government and its state-run subsidiaries retain a roster of around 145 registered agents seeking to influence American public policy.

Less scrutinized, however, are Aramco companies that have a seat at the table with other US oil giants seeking to influence domestic energy policies. Aramco owns several refineries and chemical plants, including the largest North American oil refinery, in Port Arthur, Texas, through a company it controls called Motiva Enterprises. The Aramco-owned subsidiary also sells gasoline through Shell-branded gas stations throughout the southeast.

Motiva, like other oil majors, shapes the energy debate largely through industry trade groups. The company is a dues-paying member of the American Fuel & Petrochemical Manufacturers, a trade group for oil refiners.

Brian Coffman, the president of Motiva, has a seat on AFPM's board. Other refinery companies, including Koch Industries, Valero Energy, Marathon Petroleum, and ExxonMobil, are also members of AFPM, providing the group with $31 million a year to advance the industry's interests. AFPM referred questions about Motiva's role in the trade group to Motiva, which did not respond to a request for comment.

Last year, AFPM played a critical role in defeating Washington State ballot Initiative 1631, a state referendum designed to institute a carbon tax. AFPM gave $1.25 million to the opposition campaign, which used the money to barrage voters with advertisements urging defeat of the measure.

AFPM, notably, has also bankrolled many of the groups that have played a vital role in the discourse around climate science. AFPM provides $75,000 a year to the Heartland Institute, an extremist think tank known for declaring that there is no human cause or evidence for climate change. The think tank once sponsored a billboard campaign comparing those concerned about climate change to the Unabomber and Osama bin Laden.

AFPM funds, using member oil company money, also flow to other groups that have lobbied against renewable energy policies. AFPM funds the American Legislative Exchange Council, the Competitive Enterprise Institute, and the American Energy Alliance. All three groups have advocated against climate-friendly policies such as the low carbon fuel standard and the enactment of carbon trading programs.

Aramco is also a major board member to the American Petroleum Institute, the powerful oil lobbying group with vast influence in Washington, D.C. API, as it's known, sponsors television advertisements, employs lobbyists, and maintains close ties with the Trump administration. A recent investigation found that both AFPM and API are deeply involved in a state-based effort to obstruct electric vehicle investments.

In recent months, Aramco, through its Motiva subsidiary, has hired the Nickles Group, the lobbying firm founded by former Republican Sen. Don Nickles, to influence regulatory policy. Its team has focused on the renewable fuel standard, a contentious law that requires refineries to blend ethanol or to buy credits from other refiners. Aramco also funds a variety of Beltway think tanks, including the Center for International Strategic Studies, a moderate group that promotes maintaining the US strategic alliance with Saudi Arabia.

Preparing for Extreme Climate

Even as they push back against efforts to reduce emissions during climate negotiations, the Saudis are girding themselves for them in other arenas. With the expected increase of electric vehicles, Saudi Aramco is preparing to shift away from crude oil and into petrochemicals. The state oil company announced in March that it would be buying a controlling stake in Sabic, the Saudi plastics manufacturer, to utilize non-carbon-intensive products for its petroleum wealth.

While derailing international and US domestic efforts to address climate change, Saudi Arabia is already experiencing some of its worst effects. The record high temperatures throughout the Arabian peninsula this summer will increasingly become the norm, according to researchers, making parts of the country and the entire Middle East region uninhabitable.

Meanwhile, to the west on the Red Sea coast, the Saudi city of Jeddah has begun flooding yearly. Saudi Arabia is ranked among the most "water stressed" countries in the world—a predicament it deals with by using both fossil fuel profits and fossil fuels themselves to desalinate and pump seawater.

Developing Countries Can't Afford Climate Change

Tucker Davey

Tucker Davey is a writer and researcher at the Future of Life Institute. He focuses on issues related to climate change and artificial intelligence.

Developing countries currently cannot sustain themselves, let alone grow, without relying heavily on fossil fuels. Global warming typically takes a back seat to feeding, housing, and employing these countries' citizens. Yet the weather fluctuations and consequences of climate change are already impacting food growth in many of these countries. Is there a solution?

Developing Countries Need Fossil Fuels

Fossil fuels are still the cheapest, most reliable energy resources available. When a developing country wants to build a functional economic system and end rampant poverty, it turns to fossil fuels.

India, for example, is home to one-third of the world's 1.2 billion citizens living in poverty. That's 400 million people in one country without sufficient food or shelter (for comparison, the entire US population is roughly 323 million people). India hopes to transition to renewable energy as its economy grows, but the investment needed to meet its renewable energy goals "is equivalent to over four times the country's annual defense spending, and over ten times the country's annual spending on health and education."

Unless something changes, developing countries like India cannot fight climate change and provide for their citizens. In fact, developing countries will only accelerate global warming as their economies grow because they cannot afford alternatives. Wealthy

"Developing Countries Can't Afford Climate Change," by Tucker Davey, Future of Life Institute, August 5, 2016. Reprinted by permission.

countries cannot afford to ignore the impact of these growing, developing countries.

The Link Between Economic Growth and CO_2

According to a World Bank report, "poor and middle-income countries already account for just over half of total carbon emissions." And this percentage will only rise as developing countries grow. Achieving a global society in which all citizens earn a living wage and climate catastrophe is averted requires breaking the link between economic growth and increasing carbon emissions in developing countries.

Today, most developing countries that decrease their poverty rates also have increased rates of carbon emissions. In East Asia and the Pacific, the number of people living in extreme poverty declined from 1.1 billion to 161 million between 1981 and 2011—an 85% decrease. In this same time period, the amount of carbon dioxide per capita rose from 2.1 tons per capita to 5.9 tons per capita—a 185% increase.

South Asia saw similar changes during this time frame. As the number of people living in extreme poverty decreased by 30%, the amount of carbon dioxide increased by 204%.

In Sub-Saharan Africa, the number of people living in poverty increased by 98% in this thirty-year span, while carbon dioxide per capita decreased by 17%. Given the current energy situation, if sub-Saharan Africans are to escape extreme poverty, they will have to increase their carbon use—unless developed countries step in to offer clean alternatives.

Carbon Emissions Rate vs. Total

Many wealthier countries have been researching alternative forms of energy for decades. And that work may be starting to pay off.

New data shows that, since the year 2000, 21 developed countries have reduced annual greenhouse gas emissions while simultaneously growing their economies. Moreover, this isn't all related to a drop in the industrial sector. Uzbekistan, Bulgaria,

Switzerland, and the Czech Republic demonstrated that countries do not need to shrink their industrial sectors to break the link between economic growth and increased greenhouse gas emissions.

Most importantly, global carbon emissions stalled from 2014 to 2015 as the global economy grew.

But is this rate of global decoupling fast enough to keep the planet from warming another two degrees Celsius? When emissions stall at 32.1 billion metric tons for two years, that's still 64.2 billion metric tons of carbon being pumped into the atmosphere over two years.

The carbon emissions rate might fall, but the total continues to grow enormously. A sharp decline in carbon emissions is necessary to keep the planet at a safe global temperature. At the 2015 Paris Climate Conference, the United Nations concluded that in order to keep global temperatures from rising another two degrees Celsius, global carbon emissions "must fall to net zero in the second half of the century."

In order to encourage this, the Paris agreement included measures to ensure that wealthy countries finance developing countries "with respect to both mitigation and adaptation." For mitigation, countries are expected to abide by their pledges to reduce emissions and use more renewable energy, and for adaptation, the deal sets a global goal for "enhancing adaptive capacity, strengthening resilience and reducing vulnerability to climate change."

Incentivizing R&D

One way wealthy countries can benefit both themselves and developing countries is through research and development. As wealthier countries develop cheaper forms of alternative energy, developing countries can take advantage of the new technologies. Wealthy countries can also help subsidize renewable energy for countries dealing with higher rates of poverty.

Yet, as of 2014, wealthy countries had invested very little in this process, providing only 0.2% of developing countries' GDP for adaptation and mitigation. Moreover, a 2015 paper from the IMF revealed that while we spend $100 billion per year subsidizing renewable energy, we spend an estimated $5.3 trillion subsidizing fossil fuels. This fossil fuel subsidy includes "the uncompensated costs of air pollution, congestion and global warming."

Such a huge disparity indicates that wealthy countries either need stronger incentives or stronger legal obligations to shift this fossil fuel money towards renewable energy. The Paris agreement intends to strengthen legal obligations, but its language is vague, and it lacks details that would ensure wealthy countries follow through with their responsibilities.

However, despite the shortcomings of legal obligations, monetary incentives do exist. India, for example, wants to vastly increase its solar power capacity to address this global threat. They need $100 billion to fund this expansion, which could spell a huge opportunity for US banks, according to Raymond Vickery, an expert on US-India economic ties. This would be a boon for the US economy, and it would set an important precedent for other wealthy countries to assist and invest in developing countries.

However, global leaders need to move quickly. The effects of global warming already threaten the world and the economies of developing countries, especially India.

Global Impact of Climate Change

India relies on the monsoon cycle to water crops and maintain its "nearly $370 billion agricultural sector and hundreds of millions of jobs." Yet as the Indian Ocean has warmed, the monsoon cycle has become unreliable, resulting in massive droughts and dying crops.

Across the globe, scientists expect developing countries such as India to be hit hardest by rising temperatures and changes in rainfall. Furthermore, these countries with limited financial resources and weak infrastructure will struggle to adapt and sustain their economic growth in the face of changing climate. Nicholas Stern predicts that a two-degree rise in temperature would cost about 1% of world GDP. But the World Bank estimates that it would cost India 5% of their GDP.

Moreover, changes such as global warming act as "threat multipliers" because they increase the likelihood of other existential threats. In India, increased carbon dioxide emissions have contributed to warmer temperatures, which have triggered extensive droughts and increased poverty. But the problems don't end here. Higher levels of hunger and poverty can magnify political tensions, potentially leading to conflict and even nuclear war. India and Pakistan both have nuclear weapons—if drought expands and cripples their economies, violence can more easily erupt.

Alternatively, wealthy nations could capitalize on investment opportunities in developing countries. In doing so, their own economies will benefit while simultaneously aiding the effort to reach net zero carbon emissions.

Global warming is, by definition, a global crisis. Mitigating this threat will require global cooperation and global solutions.

Corruption Limits the Effect of a Green Economy

Leslie Forsyth

Leslie Forsyth is a writer and the executive director at Foro Nacional Internacional.

While climate change is a global challenge, it has a greater impact in developing countries. Many emerging economies depend economically and culturally on natural resources, ecosystems and the environment, which leaves them especially vulnerable to climate-related storms, droughts, floods and other extreme weather.

Natural disasters, changes in ecosystems and loss of biodiversity are constant threats for developing countries, that require robust policy and effective implementation. But most developing countries have fairly fragile governments and institutions, and are especially vulnerable to corruption and mismanagement.

Free and open democracies usually are better able to implement mitigation and adaption strategies for climate change (Povitkina 2018), as they are more involved in international environmental treaties, and have an enabling ecosystem of civil society, multilateral organisations and environmental awareness created by free media, playing an important role in the adoption of environmental policies.

Despite this, these benefits are limited by the presence of business interests which have an out-sized influence on political decisions. Corruption and political capture can also obstruct effective climate policy, limiting the quality of inspections, design and implementation of policies, and monitoring, among others.

Solving environmental problems depends, to a great extent, on the quality and strength of institutions, and the capacity of civil society to supervise. Fragile governments present a major challenge for addressing climate change and corruption. This is a serious obstacle for aid agencies and the allocation of funding, as in some cases besides promoting climate change strategies, an anti-corruption parallel plan has to be implemented to assure positive outcomes.

Corruption is defined by Transparency International as "the abuse of entrusted power for private gain." But as the UN points out, it's important to understand that corruption can take place in both the public and private sector, and even between them. Corruption and climate change share a characteristic: both are most devastating for the poor and vulnerable people as they have less access and control of resources. For this reason, it is urgent to strengthen institutions and create a more vigilant civil society.

The Peruvian Case

The adoption of the 2030 Agenda for Sustainable Development and the Paris Agreements on climate change are starting to lead Peru to adopt certain plans, actions and strategies that should, in turn, lead to more inclusive and sustainable development, supported by a green economy. Reducing corruption is vital to Peru's sustainable development goals as it presents a major obstacle for development and ending extreme poverty.

Thanks to the international Odebrecht scandal, corruption has recently been revealed as a major threat to all dimensions of Peruvian government, involving congresspersons, the judiciary, regional governors, and 3 elected presidents—many of whom are facing charges or being sentenced. This affects the enforcement of regulation and legislation intended to protect resources and ecological systems. These actions are generally related to logging, mining and the extraction of other resources under the payment of bribes—in other words, an enormous threat to the environment.

Illegal logging is a serious issue in Peru, where 90% of forested land in Peru is classified as primary rainforest. In the Amazon region there is little supervision from authorities, as well as a lack of resources and capacity to confront this problem. Organised crime, money laundering and a thriving black market in permits and paperwork allow illegal timber to evade environmental safeguards and create huge profits.

This system allows the devastation of enormous territories, undermining communities whose livelihoods depend on these forests. The Peruvian region of Madre de Dios loses approximately4,437 hectares of forest every year, so solutions for sustainable results are desperately needed to prevent the logging.

Illegal mining is also devastating forests and communities in Peru, as well as driving human trafficking. A rush to mine gold reserves is destroying important forest reserves as well as contaminating rivers, soil and whole ecosystems, releasing tonnes of mercury into the river and devastating the surroundings and being extremely harmful for people's health.

This situation has been going on for several years under the watch and, in some cases, involvement and consent of regional governors and judges. Despite efforts to stop this devastation, miners are often tipped off about government interventions allowing them to escape before the police arrive. Corruption is thus directly driving the destruction of the Amazon rainforest.

Conclusions

Sadly, even well-meaning attempts to assist emerging economies with climate adaptation and mitigation strategies can be subverted; development aid and financial assistance is easily siphoned off by corrupt institutions. Even emergency relief aid in the wake of environmental crises or climate disasters is ripe for corruption. Urgent efforts are therefore required to achieve transparency, accountability and integrity as a first step towards sustainable development. It is crucial that climate money get to where it is most needed: the communities, policies, and infrastructure for climate change adaptation.

Chapter 3

Will Switching to a Green Economy Solve Climate Change?

Overview: Carbon Emissions Goals and the Green Economy

Carolyn Kormann

Carolyn Kormann is a staff writer at the New Yorker. *Her area of specialization is green energy and the environment.*

In 1974, the economist William Nordhaus described the transition from a "cowboy economy" to a "spaceship economy." In the former, he wrote, "we could afford to use our resources profligately," and "the environment could be used as a sink without becoming fouled." But, in the spaceship economy, "great attention must be paid to the sources of life and to the dumps where our refuse is piled." He added, "Things which have traditionally been treated as free goods—air, water, quiet, natural beauty—must now be treated with the same care as other scarce goods." Toward the end of his landmark paper, "Resources as a Constraint on Growth," Nordhaus discussed the possible adverse effects of energy consumption, most notably the "greenhouse effect." From a "rough calculation," he found that the atmospheric concentration of carbon dioxide would increase by more than forty per cent in the next sixty years. "Although this is below the fateful doubling of CO_2 concentration," he wrote—scientists had already predicted that such a doubling could cause the polar ice caps to melt catastrophically—"it may well be too close for comfort." He was prescient. We are now dangerously on track to hit his estimate, four hundred and eighty-seven parts per million, by 2030.

In the United States, after three years of decline, carbon-dioxide emissions increased by an estimated 3.4 per cent in 2018, according to a report released earlier this month by the Rhodium Group, a private climate-research firm. The authors blame two main factors: a particularly cold winter and fast economic growth. In

"The False Choice Between Economic Growth and Combatting Climate Change," by Carolyn Kormann, the *New Yorker*, February 4, 2019. Reprinted by permission.

the past two decades, the only greater annual gain in emissions was in 2010, when the economy was rebounding from the Great Recession. Historically, emissions have aligned with the ebb and flow of the economy. In 2018, economic growth was driven by a higher demand for energy, trucking and air travel, and industrial activity. Companies were manufacturing more stuff, including steel, cement, and chemicals. The carbon intensity of the power sector, meanwhile, did not decline fast enough to offset all those demand increases. As has been common since Nordhaus's 1974 paper, the report seems to pit controlling climate change against a growing global economy.

The picture could have been much different. Nordhaus went on to publish a series of foundational studies on the economics of climate change. In 1992, he created an integrated economic and scientific model that could be used to determine the most efficient ways to cut greenhouse-gas emissions. His work—and that of many other economists who followed his lead—showed that a low tax on carbon, set to rise slowly over time, could be enough to keep emissions at reasonable levels, saving us from climate change at little, if any, cost. A "spaceship economy" could thrive if governments made sure that companies paid an appropriate price for the environmental damage they caused—what would come to be called the social cost of carbon. Companies that were most easily able to reduce their level of pollution would be incentivized to make the greatest reductions, and to invest in cheaper and better pollution-reduction systems. The dirtiest activities would be the most costly. The tax would promote innovations in new forms of power generation and, eventually, a widespread adoption of clean-energy technologies. The way to break the chain was to reimagine how we fuel the global economy. "It's absolutely the case that emissions and growth can be decoupled," Marshall Burke, an assistant professor in Stanford University's Department of Earth System Science, told me. He pointed to research plotting how thirty-five countries, including the United States, did, in fact, experience economic growth in the past fifteen years while reducing their emissions—and not solely due to recessions. But the decline was not nearly enough. "The technology is available to have faster economic growth while reducing over-all emissions," Trevor Houser, the head of Rhodium Group's energy and climate team, and one of the authors of the report, told me. But the switch to nuclear and renewables needs to happen more rapidly. "It takes policy. It won't happen through markets alone," Houser said.

In October, Nordhaus and another economist, Paul Romer, won the Nobel Prize in Economic Sciences for, respectively, "integrating climate change" and "technological innovations" into "long-run macroeconomic analysis." The timing of the announcement from Sweden was painfully ironic. Hours earlier, the United Nations had released its dire report warning that, if climate change's worst impacts were to be avoided, the nations of the world had about a decade to revolutionize the energy economy. "The policies are lagging very, very far—miles, miles, miles behind the science and what needs to be done," Nordhaus said after receiving the prize. "It's hard to be optimistic . . . We're actually going backward in the United States, with the disastrous policies of the Trump Administration." The Obama Administration had, in its final years, partially incorporated concepts that Nordhaus had helped to develop, such as putting a price on the economic harm that results from every additional ton of carbon dioxide emitted into the atmosphere. The price was set at forty-five dollars a ton, and used in both regulatory cost-benefit analyses, which undergirded new fuel-efficiency standards, and the Clean Power Plan, which would have propelled a faster retirement of coal-powered electric plants and a broader transition to renewables. Just as such policies were "beginning to bear fruit," Houser said, "that whole framework was dismantled." Under Trump, the social cost of a ton of carbon is as little as one dollar.

As emissions keep growing, and climate change advances, there is less and less time to make the necessary cuts. "The pace we needed to decline was already much larger than what was happening," Houser told me. "Now we have to go even faster to meet our Paris Agreement target by 2025"—on average, a 2.6-per-cent reduction in annual energy-related carbon-dioxide emissions in the next seven years. "That is considerably faster than at any point in history," he said. And it will need to go even faster if declines in other greenhouse gases, including methane and hydrofluorocarbons—which endure in the atmosphere for much shorter amounts of time than carbon dioxide but are much more potent—do not keep pace.

A modest carbon tax of the sort Nordhaus proposed decades ago—one that was then palatable to conservatives—will therefore no longer bring us anywhere near the Paris Agreement targets. But it's one of many weapons in the arsenal that policymakers need to employ. "The real challenge is finding ways to reduce emissions and maintain economic growth on the timeline demanded by the nature of climate change," Kenneth Gillingham, an associate professor of economics at Yale University, told me. But, as much as the costs of climate mitigation will undoubtedly increase, the question is whether the benefits of mitigation exceed those costs. "It's a straw man—and terrible economics—to just point out the costs while ignoring the benefits," Burke said. He and two co-authors published a paper in *Nature* last May that shows that the economic benefits of mitigation are going to be much larger than previously believed. Cooler temperatures would help maintain and grow productivity, and reducing carbon emissions means reducing air pollution—specifically particulate matter, or soot—which brings immediate health benefits. They found that keeping global warming to one and a half degrees Celsius (which is nearly impossible at this point), as opposed to two degrees Celsius, would potentially save more than twenty trillion dollars around the world by the end of the century, and significantly reduce global inequality. Beyond two degrees, they wrote, "we find considerably greater reductions in global economic output." If nations met their commitments under the Paris Agreement, the world would still see the average global temperature rise by two and a half to three degrees Celsius, which, according to Burke's paper, would result in a fifteen-to-twenty-five-per-cent reduction in per capita output by 2100. "To just complain about the costs of this transition and ignore the benefits, as is common in the discussion from this Administration," Burke said, "is some pretty poor cost-benefit analysis from an Administration that prides itself on economic savvy."

As a small but growing coalition of congressional Democrats, led by Representative Alexandria Ocasio-Cortez, have outlined as part of their Green New Deal, transforming the energy sector—and, really, the entire economy, in a just and more equitable way—will require some sort of carbon tax (preferably a "fee and dividend" approach, which distributes tax revenues as rebates directly to citizens), and also new regulations and huge investments. "We can decarbonize the electric sector at a fairly low cost," Gillingham told me. "That's where some of the cheapest emissions reductions are to be found." Extensive government subsidies could hasten the spread of renewables—specifically, solar, wind, and batteries—and offset any rise in emissions elsewhere. As Gillingham said, "We might want to be careful about fighting climate change by preventing people from staying warm in the winter. If a winter is really cold enough, emissions increases are to be expected." Still, there are ways to reduce the use of fossil fuels in heating; utilities, for instance, can create incentive programs so that homeowners have a motivation to replace their boilers with electric heat pumps.

Houser told me that total emissions are expected to remain flat in 2019. Economists and other market observers predict that over-all economic growth will be slower, and the full impact of recent cuts to coal-plant capacity (2018 was a near-record year) has not yet been recorded. Still, in the absence of major policy changes—which is mostly dependent on a new President who makes climate policy a top and urgent priority—there is almost no chance that the US will achieve the average emissions cuts necessary to meet the Paris targets by 2025. Houser told me that our only hope would be extremely favorable market and technological conditions. "If, over the next couple of years, no more nuclear power plants retired"—more than a dozen are scheduled to retire in the next seven years—"wind, solar, and battery prices fall far faster than the currently most optimistic projections estimate, it is possible that we could come pretty close to meeting the Paris Agreement targets," he said. States, cities, and private organizations would also have to pick up a tremendous amount of slack from Washington. Even warmer winters would help. "Everything would really have to light up in the right direction," Houser said. "It's also, of course, possible that, if there was a massive global recession, we'd see a significant decline, too. But that's not the reason we want emissions to decline."

Climate Change and Its Associate Problems and Solutions

Kimberly Amadeo

Kimberly Amadeo is the president of WorldMoneyWatch and an economic expert.

Climate change is the disruption in the long-term seasonal weather patterns that are caused by global warming. The average temperature has risen around 1 degree Celsius, or 1.9 degrees Fahrenheit, since 1880.[1] That's faster than at any other time in the Earth's history.[2]

Temperatures aren't rising uniformly. The temperatures in the Arctic and Antarctic are rising faster than those in temperate and tropical areas. As a result, portions of the polar vortex have split off and blocked the jet stream. That's a river of wind high in the atmosphere that races from west to east at speeds up to 275 miles an hour. It's made the jet stream wobble.[3,4]

Climate change should be called climate destabilization. It's created more extreme and frequent blizzards, heat waves, and other forms of extreme weather. This extreme category includes tornados, wildfires, hurricanes, blizzards, floods and landslides, heat waves, and droughts. It also includes violent storms, whether they be dust, hail, rain, snow, or ice.

A 2017 poll showed that 55% of Americans believe that climate change made hurricanes worse.[5] And among adult respondents to a 2019 poll who lived in an area affected by hurricanes, 63% considered climate change to be a major factor.[6] In another 2019 poll, 57.2% of respondents reported being afraid or very afraid of global warming and climate change.[7]

Climate change is indeed nothing new in Earth's history. But previous changes occurred over millions of years, not decades.

"Climate Change Facts and Effect on the Economy," by Kimberly Amadeo, Dotdash Publishing Family, January 27, 2020. Reprinted by permission.

What Causes Climate Change?

Global warming is the planet's response to higher levels of greenhouse gases in the atmosphere. They create a blanket that traps the heat from the sun and sends it back to the planet's surface. Humans have contributed to the current crisis by burning fossil fuels that emit greenhouse gases.

As of May 2020, NASA-recorded carbon dioxide levels were 414 parts per million (ppm).[8] The last time levels were this high was 2.6 million years ago during the Pliocene era. Back then, the Arctic was 8 degrees Celsius, or 14 degrees Fahrenheit, warmer in the summer than it is now.[9] As a result, it was only frozen during the winter. With less ice, sea levels were about 25 meters higher than today.[10] That's enough to flood New York, London, Miami, San Francisco, and Shanghai.

Why isn't the Earth as hot as it was then? Greenhouse gases have risen so fast that temperatures haven't had a chance to catch up. In 1880, they were just 280 ppm.[11]

In addition, the oceans absorbed most of the added CO_2 from the atmosphere. In response, they've become 30% more acidic since the beginning of the Industrial Revolution.[12] This imbalance is causing a mass extinction of sea life. For example, around half of the world's coral reefs have died in the last 30 years.[13]

In addition to absorbing CO_2, the oceans have also absorbed 90% of the heat.[14] When water heats, it expands. That's caused rising sea levels and flooding.

The top 2,300 feet of the ocean has warmed more than 0.4 degrees since 1969.[15] The last time the ocean was this warm was 100,000 years ago. Sea levels were 20 to 30 feet higher.[16] The ocean has warmed so fast that there hasn't been enough time for higher temperatures to melt the arctic ice caps. As it does, sea levels will catch up to where they were last time the ocean was this warm. That's enough to flood New York, London, and Miami.[17]

Global warming will continue even if no more greenhouse gases were emitted starting tomorrow. The temperature is reacting to the greenhouse gases that have already been emitted. These gases must be absorbed from the atmosphere and put back into the ground to stop the effects of climate change.[18]

On Nov. 3, 2017, the Trump administration released a report that blamed climate change on human activity.[19] According to the Environmental Protection Agency, the US sources in 2018 were electricity generation, transportation, industry, commercial and residential, agriculture, and forestry. You can see the breakdown below.[20]

Source	Fuel	Percent
Electricity Generation	Coal, Natural Gas	26.9%
Transportation	Oil, Gasoline	28.2%
Industry	Oil, Chemicals	22.0%
Commercial and Residential	Heating Oil	12.3%
Agriculture	Livestock	9.9%
Forestry	Absorbs CO_2	offset 11.6%

On a per-person basis, the US is one of the worst offenders. In 2017, it emitted 14.6 metric tons of CO_2 per person. Saudi Arabia, Australia, and Canada led the world in per capita emissions, with 16.1, 15.6, and 14.9 metric tons, respectively. China emitted only 6.5 metric tons per person.[21]

Since 1751, the US has contributed 400 billion metric tons of carbon dioxide. That's a fourth of total greenhouse gases.[22] The good news is that its emissions are leveling off. The bad news is that about 20% of that will remain in the atmosphere for tens of thousands of years.[23,24]

The US is one of the world's richest countries. A recent study found that the planet's wealthiest 1 billion people emit 60% of greenhouse gases. The poorest 3 billion produce only 5%.[25] That's why you may hear people say income inequality can cause climate change.

What's the Economic Impact of Climate Change?

Insurance

From 1980 to 2019, extreme weather cost $1.775 trillion.[26] Munich Re, one of the world's largest reinsurance firms, blamed climate change for $24 billion of losses in the California wildfires.[27] It warned that insurance firms would have to raise premiums to cover rising costs from extreme weather. That could make insurance too expensive for most people.

GDP

Scientists estimated that, if temperatures only rose 2 degrees Celsius, the global gross domestic product would fall 15%. If temperatures rose to 3 degrees Celsius, the global GDP would fall 25%. If nothing is done, temperatures will rise by 4 degrees Celsius by 2100.[28,29] Global GDP would decline by more than 30% from 2010 levels.[30] That's comparable to the Great Depression, where GDP fell to -26.7%.[31] The only difference is that it would be permanent.

Employment

The World Employment and Social Outlook 2018 estimated that climate change threatens 1.2 billion jobs.[32]

The industries most at risk are agriculture, fisheries, and forestry. Maine has already seen a decline in its lobster catches.[33] Natural disasters caused or compounded by humans cost 23 million working-life years annually from 2000 to 2015.[34] On the other hand, efforts to stop climate change would create 24 million new jobs by 2030.[35,36]

Immigration

Climate change creates mass migration around the world. People are leaving flooded coastlines, drought-stricken farmlands, and areas of extreme natural disasters. Since 2008, events related to climate or weather have displaced 22.5 million people annually, according to the United Nations High Commissioner for Refugees.[37,38] Some forecasts predict that by 2050, climate change could cause as many as 1 billion people to emigrate.[39,40]

Immigration at the US border can be expected to increase as climate change worsens conditions in Latin America. The World Bank estimates that as many as 3.9 million people in Mexico and Central America will migrate internally by 2050 due to climate impact, and that subsequent deterioration will further exacerbate the movements of these migrants.[41] Drought, shifting rain patterns, and extreme weather destroys crops and leads to food insecurity. The World Food Program found that almost half of Central Americans left because there wasn't enough food.[42]

National Security

In 2017, Congress proclaimed that "climate change is a direct threat to the national security of the United States." Climate change endangers 128 military bases.[43] A 2018 Pentagon survey revealed that US Naval Academy in Annapolis, Maryland has experienced storm surge flooding and hurricane damage. The Cape Lisburne Long Range Radar Station in Alaska has lost a seawall from extreme weather.[44] In response, Congress asked the Department of Defense to identify the 10 most vulnerable sites and recommend solution strategies.[45]

Food Prices

As America experiences more extremely hot days, food prices are rising. Corn and soybean yields in the US precipitously plummet when temperatures rise above 84 degrees Fahrenheit.[46] Those crops feed cattle and other meat sources and create spikes in beef, milk, and poultry prices. Worker productivity declines sharply, particularly for outdoor jobs.[47] That further increases the cost of food.

A 2019 study found that a warming ocean has pushed global sustainable fish yields down 4% since 1930. That's 1.4 million metric tons. In the North Sea and Sea of Japan, that decline is 35%. That affects Atlantic cod, haddock, and herring.[48] Many species are threatened with extinction. That affects the 3 billion people who rely on fish for their primary source of protein.[49] It also affects the $150 billion fishing industry and the 59 million people employed.[50] It especially affects the US, which imports more than 80% of its seafood.[51]

Are There Solutions to Climate Change?

The United Nations recommended that the world limit its average temperature to 2 degrees Celsius above pre-industrial levels.[52] It's already surpassed 1 degree Celsius.[53] Here's a timeline of what's been done.

1992

The United Nations Framework Convention on Climate Change was formed.[54]

Dec. 11, 1997

The United Nations adopted the Kyoto Protocol.[55] The European Community and 37 industrialized countries promised to reduce greenhouse gas emissions between 2008 and 2012. The first commitment was to 5% below 1990 levels.[56] The second commitment period was from 2013 to 2020. They agreed to reduce emissions by 18% below 1990 levels.[57] The United States never ratified it.[58]

2008

The International Energy Agency called for countries to spend $45 trillion by 2050 to prevent greenhouse gas emissions from slowing economic growth. To put this into perspective, the gross domestic product of the entire world was about $142 trillion in 2019.[59] The measures included building 32 nuclear power plants each year and reducing greenhouse gases by 50% by 2050. This infrastructure would cost the world $100 billion to $200 billion a year for the next 10 years after 2008, and rise to $1 trillion to $2 trillion after that.[60]

Dec. 7, 2009

The Environmental Protection Agency found that concentrations of greenhouse gases threatened public health. Based on this study, the EPA finalized emission standards for cars in 2010 and trucks in 2011.[61]

Dec. 18, 2009

The UN Climate Summit produced the Copenhagen Accord.[62] Countries pledged to limit global temperature increases to 2C over the pre-industrial level. The developed countries agreed to pay $100 billion a year by 2020 to assist poor countries affected the most by climate change. That includes assistance for reducing emissions from deforestation. The countries agreed to provide $30 billion over the following three years, 2010-2012.[63] Some countries refused to sign the agreement because the United States refused to cut more than 4% of its emissions by 2020.[64] That foot-dragging signaled to many that Obama was not any more committed than the Bush administration.

2010

China promised it would reach four climate goals by 2020. These include:

1. Reduce CO_2 emissions by 40% below 2005 levels (97% achieved in 2017).
2. Increase renewable energy consumption from 9.4% to 15% (60% achieved).
3. Increase forest stock by 1.3 billion cubic meters (exceeded as of 2017).
4. Increase forest coverage by 40 million hectares relative to 2005 (60% achieved).[65]

Aug. 3, 2015

President Obama released the Clean Power Plan. It established state targets to reduce carbon emissions from power plants by 32% below 2005 levels. The goal is to do so by 2030.[66] The Trump administration seeks to replace the plan with one that focuses only on emissions from coal plants.[67]

Dec. 12, 2015

In 2015, 195 countries signed The Paris Climate Accord.[68] The United States pledged to cut greenhouse gas emissions by 26 to 28% below 2005 levels by 2025.[69,70] They also committed $3 billion in aid for poorer countries by 2020. These are most likely to suffer damage from rising sea levels and other consequences of climate change.

The Accord's goal is to keep global warming from rising 2 degrees Celsius above pre-industrial levels.[71] Many experts consider that the tipping point. Beyond that, and climate change becomes unstoppable.[72]

The United States is responsible for 20% of the world's greenhouse gas emissions.[73] It would be difficult for the other signatories to reach the Accord's goal without US participation. But they are trying. More than 60 jurisdictions around the world have carbon pricing initiatives such as carbon taxes and tradable allowances.[74] Germany, Sweden, and Denmark are considering a tax on beef.[75] Greenhouse gas emissions from livestock contribute 14.5% of the world's total.[76]

Even if all countries follow the Accord, temperatures will continue to rise. The atmosphere is still reacting to the CO_2 that's already been pumped into it. Greenhouse gases have been added so quickly that temperatures haven't caught up yet.

As a result, measures need to be stricter to reverse global warming. The Climate Impact Lab predicts major cities will see many days above 95 degrees Fahrenheit.[77] By 2100, Washington D.C. will experience 29 extremely hot days each year. That's quadruple the average of seven it experienced from 1986 to 2005.

Nov. 4, 2016

The Paris Agreement went into force as 55 members ratified the agreement. They make up 55% of global emissions.[78,79]

June 1, 2017
President Trump announced the United States would withdraw from the Paris Accord. Trump said he wanted to negotiate a better deal. Leaders from Germany, France, and Italy said the Accord is non-negotiable. China and India joined the other leaders in stating they remain committed to the Accord.[80] Some have argued that America's withdrawal from a leadership position creates a vacuum that China will readily fill. The United States cannot legally exit until Nov. 4, 2020.[81] This timing makes it an issue for the 2020 presidential election.

Business leaders from Tesla, General Electric, and Goldman Sachs denounced the withdrawal. US companies need government support and subsidies in these industries to pay for research and bring costs down.

China is already taking the lead in electric vehicles. Almost half of the world's plug-in electric vehicles are sold in China.[82] Its regulations and subsidies drive consumers away from gasoline-powered cars. China wants to reduce pollution. It also wants to reduce reliance on foreign oil. But more importantly, it wants to improve the country's automakers. China's car market is large and is forcing foreign carmakers to improve electric vehicle production.

Oct. 10, 2017
The Trump administration proposed to repeal the Clean Power Plan.

Nov. 8, 2017
The European Union agreed to cut carbon-dioxide emissions by new vehicles by 30% between 2021 and 2030.[83]

Dec. 12, 2017
French President Emmanuel Macron convened world leaders to the One Planet Summit. Macron told *TIME* that Trump was not invited because he withdrew from the Accord.[84] The summit focused on how to finance the global transition away from fossil fuels.

September 2018

A team of administrative appointees submitted to the governor of Alaska its detailed action plan for addressing climate change. Even though it is a major oil producer, it's feeling the effects of global warming. The permafrost is thawing, destabilizing roads, and buildings that sit on it. Protective sea ice is melting, allowing powerful waves to erode Alaskan shores. As a result, 31 coastal towns may need to relocate.[85]

The world's 1,000 biggest corporations contribute 12% of greenhouse gas emissions. In 2017, 89% had plans to cut those emissions. But it's not enough to reach the U.N.'s target of 2 degrees Celsius. Fourteen percent of the companies already achieved or had goals to align with that target. Another 30% pledged to do so in the following two years.[86] Investment firms, such as HSBC Holdings and Goldman Sachs, have begun targeting more low-carbon businesses.

Republican Newt Gingrich, the former Speaker of the House, argued for the importance of supporting entrepreneurial environmental solutions in his 2007 book, *A Contract with the Earth*.[87] Pressure on the market forces that got the atmosphere into trouble is the best solution to clean it up.

7 Steps You Can Take to Help Stop Climate Change

Until there is stronger government leadership, we must create our progress. Many everyday citizens and entrepreneurs are hard at work on innovative ways to address climate change.

First, plant trees and other vegetation to halt deforestation. You can also donate to charities that plant trees. For example, Eden Reforestation hires residents to plant trees in Madagascar, Haiti, Nepal, Indonesia, Mozambique, Kenya, and Central America for $0.10 a tree. It also gives the very poor people an income, rehabilitates their habitat, and saves species from mass extinction.[88,89]

Second, become carbon neutral. The average American emitted 14.6 tons of CO_2 in 2017.[90] According to Arbor Environmental

Alliance, 100 mangrove trees can absorb 2.18 metric tons of CO_2 annually. The average American would need to plant 734 mangrove trees to offset one year's worth of CO_2. At $0.10 a tree, that would cost $73.

The United Nations program Climate Neutral Now also allows you to offset your emissions by purchasing credits.[91,92] These credits fund green initiatives such as wind energy or solar power heaters in developing countries.

Third, enjoy a plant-based diet with less meat. Cows create methane, a greenhouse gas. Monoculture crops to feed the cows cause deforestation. The Drawdown Coalition estimated those forests would have absorbed 39.3 gigatons of carbon dioxide.[93] Greenpeace points out the production of these food items will create 50% of global greenhouse gas emissions by 2050.[94]

Similarly, avoid products using palm oil. Most of its production comes from Malaysia and Indonesia. Tropical forests and carbon-rich swamps are cleared for its plantations. Avoid products with generic vegetable oil as an ingredient.

Fourth, pressure corporations to disclose and act on their climate-related risks. Since 1988, 100 companies are responsible for more than 70% of greenhouse gas emissions. The worst are ExxonMobil, Shell, BP, and Chevron.[95]

Fifth, reduce food waste. The Drawdown Coalition estimated that as much as 18.8 gigatons of CO_2 emissions would be avoided if food waste was reduced by 50% by 2050.[96]

Sixth, cut fossil-fuel use. Where available, use more mass transit, biking, and electric vehicles. Or keep your car but maintain it. Keep the tires inflated, change the air filter, and drive under 60 miles per hour.

Seventh, hold the government accountable. Each year, $2 trillion is invested in building new energy infrastructure. The International Energy Administration said that governments control 70% of that.[97]

Similarly, people can vote for candidates who promise a solution to climate change. The Sunrise Movement is pressuring candidates to adopt a Green New Deal. More than 2,500 candidates and elected officials have signed a pledge not to accept contributions over $200 from the fossil fuel industry.[98]

What's the Outlook on Climate Change?

Scientists predict that by 2050 temperatures will have caught up with today's level of CO_2.[99] That's when there will be no Arctic ice in the summer. The dark ocean that replaces it will absorb even more heat.[100] It will create a chain reaction that will further heat the Earth's temperature even if we stop emitting additional greenhouse gases.

Greenhouse gas emissions increased by 41% from 1990 to 2020. Levels dropped in 2016, but have risen since.[101,102] Power plants began switching from coal to natural gas, and a warmer winter reduced demand for heating oil.

There are no safe places in a climate-change future. Climate destabilization means that the world will be pummeled by extreme weather. Also, mass extinction threatens agriculture. A United Nations report estimates that 17% of bats and birds that pollinate are at risk, and that 75% of the world's food crops rely on pollinators to some extent.[103] If these species go extinct, so does almost 8% of the world's food production.[104] A third of the fishing areas are over harvested.[105] Everyone will be affected in ways that are difficult to imagine now.

The Bottom Line

Climate change is a global reality that must be addressed now. The colossal quantities of carbon dioxide pumped into the atmosphere over the past century are warming temperatures at a seriously rapid rate. Because of this, flooding, extreme weather, wildfires, and other natural disasters are occurring more frequently and at a greater degree of intensity than ever.

Decisive, committed actions must be taken today to avert an added temperature rise exceeding 2 degrees Celsius. This is the world's tipping point before permanent catastrophes descend and change life as we all know it. Today, we only have 0.5 degrees Celsius leeway before this happens. It's time to punch that red alert button to push everyone in the world to lower their carbon emissions now before it becomes too late.

Endnotes

1. NASA Goddard Institute for Space Studies. "New Studies Increase Confidence in NASA's Measure of Earth's Temperature." Accessed June 29, 2020.

2. NASA Earth Observatory. "If Earth Has Warmed and Cooled Throughout History, What Makes Scientists Think That Humans Are Causing Global Warming Now?" Accessed June 29, 2020.

3. Climate.gov. "Wobbly Polar Vortex Triggers Extreme Cold Air Outbreak." Accessed June 29, 2020.

4. National Weather Service. "The Jet Stream." Accessed June 29, 2020.

5. Langer Research Associates. "Most Now See Climate Change as Responsible for Hurricane Severity." Accessed June 29, 2020.

6. The *Washington Post*. "Washington Post-KFF Climate Change Survey," Page 14. Accessed June 29, 2020.

7. Chapman University. "Methodology Report: American Fears Survey," Page 43. Accessed June 29, 2020.

8. NASA. "Carbon Dioxide." Accessed June 29, 2020.

9. AAAS. "Pliocene Warmth, Polar Amplification, and Stepped Pleistocene Cooling Recorded in NE Arctic Russia." Accessed June 29, 2020.

10. Nature. "The Amplitude and Origin of Sea-Level Variability During the Pliocene Epoch." Accessed June 29, 2020.

11. National Oceanic and Atmospheric Administration. "NOAA: Carbon Dioxide Levels Reach Milestone at Arctic Sites." Accessed June 29, 2020.

12. National Oceanic and Atmospheric Administration. "Ocean Acidification Threatening Our Oceans," Pages 3, 9, 11. Accessed June 25, 2020.

13. National Academies of Sciences, Engineering, and Medicine. "Protecting Coral Reefs in a Deteriorating Environment." Accessed June 25, 2020.

14. NASA. "NASA-MIT Study Evaluates Efficiency of Oceans As Heat Sink, Atmospheric Gases Sponge." Accessed June 25, 2020.

15. NASA. "Climate Change: How Do We Know?" Accessed June 25, 2020.

16. *Science*. "Regional and Global Sea-Surface Temperatures During the Last Interglaciation." Accessed June 25, 2020.

17. NASA. "Melting Ice, Warming Ocean: Take Control in a New Simulation." Accessed June 25, 2020.

18. NASA. "Is It Too Late to Prevent Climate Change?" Accessed June 25, 2020.

19. National Oceanic and Atmospheric Administration. "Federal Climate Science Report for US Released." Accessed June 25, 2020.

20. United States Environmental Protection Agency. "Sources of Greenhouse Gas Emissions." Accessed June 25, 2020.

21. Union of Concerned Scientists. "Each Country's Share of CO_2 Emissions." Accessed June 25, 2020.

22. Our World in Data. "CO_2 and Greenhouse Gas Emissions." Accessed June 25, 2020.

23. Yale Climate Connections. "Common Climate Misconceptions: Atmospheric Carbon Dioxide." Accessed June 25, 2020.

24. The University of Chicago. "Fate of Fossil Fuel CO_2 in Geologic Time," Page 1. Accessed June 25, 2020.

25. Proceedings of the National Academy of Sciences of the United States of America. "Trajectories of the Earth System in the Anthropocene," Appendix, Page 14. Click on "Download Appendix (PDF)." Accessed June 25, 2020.

26. National Centers for Environmental Information. "Billion-Dollar Weather and Climate Disasters: Overview." Accessed June 25, 2020.

27. Munich Re. "Extreme Storms, Wildfires and Droughts Cause Heavy Nat Cat Losses in 2018." Accessed June 25, 2020.

28. *Science.* "New Climate Models Predict a Warming Surge." Accessed June 25, 2020.

29. The Intergovernmental Panel on Climate Change. "Climate Change 2014 Synthesis Report Summary for Policymakers," Page 10. Accessed June 25, 2020.

30. *Nature.* "Large Potential Reduction in Economic Damages Under UN Mitigation Targets." Accessed June 25, 2020.

31. Congressional Research Service. "The 2007–2009 Recession: Similarities to and Differences From the Past," Page 8. Accessed June 25, 2020.

32. International Labour Organization. "World Employment and Social Outlook 2018—Greening With Jobs," Pages 2, 7, 19–28. Accessed June 25, 2020.

33. Maine.gov. "Historical Maine Lobster Landings," Page 3. Accessed June 25, 2020.

34. International Labour Organization. "World Employment and Social Outlook 2018—Greening With Jobs," Pages 7, 23. Accessed June 25, 2020.

35. International Labour Organization. "World Employment and Social Outlook 2018—Greening With Jobs," Pages iii, 1, 37, 43. Accessed June 25, 2020.

36. United Nations. "Green Economy Could Create 24 Million Jobs." Accessed June 25, 2020.

37. Center for International Environmental Law. "Rising Climate-Related Displacement Highlights the Need for a Human Rights–Based Approach to Protecting Migrants." Accessed June 25, 2020.

38. UNHCR. "Environment, Disasters and Climate Change." Accessed June 25, 2020.

39. International Organization for Migration. "IOM Outlook on Migration, Environment and Climate Change," Page 38. Accessed June 25, 2020.

40. United States Government Accountability Office. "Climate Change: Activities of Selected Agencies to Address Potential Impact on Global Migration," Page 5. Accessed June 25, 2020.

41. The World Bank. "Internal Climate Migration in Latin America," Pages 3–6. Download report. Accessed June 25, 2020.

42. World Food Programme. "Food Security and Emigration," Pages 6, 13, 17. Accessed June 25, 2020.

43. Union of Concerned Scientists. "The US Military on the Front Lines of Rising Seas." Accessed June 25, 2020.

44. The Center for Climate & Security. "Department of Defense Climate-Related Risk to DoD Infrastructure Initial Vulnerability Assessment Survey," Pages 9, 10. Accessed June 25, 2020.

45. Congress.gov. "H.R.2810—National Defense Authorization Act for Fiscal Year 2018," Page 131 Stat. 1359. Accessed June 25, 2020.

46. Proceedings of the National Academy of Sciences of the United States of America. "Nonlinear Temperature Effects Indicate Severe Damages to US Crop Yields Under Climate Change." Accessed June 25, 2020.

47. SSRN. "Temperature and Economic Growth: New Evidence From Total Factor Productivity," Page 8. Download PDF. Accessed June 25, 2020.

48. *Science.* "Impacts of Historical Warming on Marine Fisheries Production." Accessed June 25, 2020.

49. *Science.* "Food Security: The Challenge of Feeding 9 Billion People." Accessed June 25, 2020.

50. Food and Agriculture Organization of the United Nations. "The State of World Fisheries and Aquaculture," Pages 2, 5, 7, 54. Accessed June 25, 2020.

51. FishWatch. "Global Wild Fisheries." Accessed June 25, 2020.

52. IPCC. "FAQ Chapter 1." Accessed June 25, 2020.

53. IPCC. "Choices Made Now Are Critical for the Future of Our Ocean and Cryosphere." Accessed June 25, 2020.

54. United Nations Climate Change. "United Nations Framework Convention on Climate Change." Accessed June 25, 2020.

55. United Nations Climate Change. "The Kyoto Protocol—Status of Ratification." Accessed June 25, 2020.

56. Eurostat. "Glossary: Kyoto Protocol." Accessed June 25, 2020.

57. United Nations Climate Change. "What Is the Kyoto Protocol?" Accessed June 25, 2020.

58. Congressional Research Service. "A US-Centric Chronology of the United Nations Framework Convention on Climate Change," Page 4. Accessed June 25, 2020.

59. Statista. "Global Gross Domestic Product (GDP) at Current Prices From 2009 to 2021." Accessed June 25, 2020.

60. IEA. "Now or Never: IEA Energy Technology Perspectives 2008 Shows Pathways to Sustained Economic Growth Based on Clean and Affordable Energy Technology." Accessed June 25, 2020.

61. United States Environmental Protection Agency. "Endangerment and Cause or Contribute Findings for Greenhouse Gases Under the Section 202(a) of the Clean Air Act." Accessed June 25, 2020.

62. United Nations Climate Change. "Information Provided by Parties to the Convention Relating to the Copenhagen Accord." Accessed June 25, 2020.

63. United Nations Climate Change. "Report of the Conference of the Parties on Its Fifteenth Session, Held in Copenhagen From 7 to 19 December 2009." Accessed June 25, 2020.

64. *Vanity Fair*. "The Ugly Truth About Obama's 'Copenhagen Accord.'" Accessed June 25, 2020.

65. World Resources Institute. "China Making Progress on Climate Goals Faster Than Expected." Accessed June 25, 2020.

66. United States Environmental Protection Agency. "Fact Sheet: Overview of the Clean Power Plan." Accessed June 25, 2020.

67. The White House. "President Trump's Energy Independence Policy." Accessed June 25, 2020.

68. United Nations Climate Change. "Paris Agreement." Accessed June 25, 2020.

69. Congressional Research Service. "US Carbon Dioxide Emissions in the Electricity Sector: Factors, Trends, and Projections," Page 1. Accessed June 25, 2020.

70. The White House, President Barack Obama. "Fact Sheet: US Reports Its 2025 Emissions Target to the UNFCCC." Accessed June 25, 2020.

71. United Nations Climate Change. "What Is the Paris Agreement?" Accessed June 25, 2020.

72. Oxford Research Encyclopedias. "The Two Degrees Celsius Limit." Accessed June 25, 2020.

73. Pew Center for Climate and Energy Solutions. "Climate Data: Insights and Observations," Page 4. Accessed June 25, 2020.

74. The World Bank. "Carbon Pricing Dashboard." Accessed June 25, 2020.

75. FAIRR. "The Livestock Levy: Are Regulators Considering Meat Taxes?" Accessed June 25, 2020.

76. Food and Agriculture Organization of the United Nations. "Key Facts and Findings." Accessed June 25, 2020.

77. Climate Impact Lab. "Assessing the Effect of Rising Temperatures," Pages 2, 7–9. Accessed June 25, 2020.

78. United Nations Treaty Collection. "Chapter XXVII Environment 7. d Paris Agreement." Accessed June 25, 2020.

79. United Nations. "Paris Climate Agreement to Enter Into Force on 4 November." Accessed June 25, 2020.

80. Council on Foreign Relations. "Role Reversal: As the United States Steps Back From Global Leadership, India Steps Up." Accessed June 25, 2020.

81. Congressional Research Service. "Withdrawal From International Agreements: Legal Framework, the Paris Agreement, and the Iran Nuclear Agreement," Page 19. Accessed June 25, 2020.

82. ZSW. "Global E-car Count Up From 3.4 to 5.6 Million." Accessed June 25, 2020.

83. European Commission. "Energy Union: Commission Takes Action to Reinforce EU's Global Leadership in Clean Vehicles." Accessed June 25, 2020.

84. *TIME.* "At Home in the World." Accessed June 25, 2020.

85. US Government Accountability Office. "Alaska Native Villages: Limited Progress Has Been Made on Relocating Villages Threatened by Flooding and Erosion." Accessed June 25, 2020.

86. CDP. "Picking Up the Pace: Analysis Shows Corporates Raising the Bar on Climate Action, As 150+ Companies Take the Top Spot on CDP's Environmental A List." Accessed June 25, 2020.

87. Amazon. "A Contract With the Earth." Accessed June 25, 2020.

88. Eden Reforestation Projects. "FAQs." Accessed June 25, 2020.

89. Eden Reforestation Projects. "Endangered Species in Madagascar." Accessed June 25, 2020.

90. Union of Concerned Scientists. "Each Country's Share of CO_2 Emissions." Accessed June 25, 2020.

91. United Nations Climate Change. "Climate Neutral Now." Accessed June 25, 2020.

92. United Nations Carbon Offset Platform. "Take Climate Action by Supporting Green Projects." Accessed June 25, 2020.

93. Google Books. "Drawdown: The Most Comprehensive Plan Ever Proposed to Reverse Global Warming," Page 40. Locate in preview window. Accessed June 25, 2020.

94. Greenpeace. "Less Is More." Accessed June 25, 2020.

95. CDP. "New Report Shows Just 100 Companies Are Source of Over 70% of Emissions." Accessed June 18, 2020.

96. Project Drawdown. "Reduced Food Waste." Accessed June 25, 2020.

97. IEA. "World Energy Outlook 2018 Examines Future Patterns of Global Energy System at a Time of Increasing Uncertainties." Accessed June 25, 2020.

98. No Fossil Fuel Money Pledge. "Pledge Signers." Accessed June 25, 2020.

99. Skeptical Science. "Climate Change: The 40 Year Delay Between Cause and Effect." Accessed June 25, 2020.

100. National Oceanic and Atmospheric Administration. "Future Arctic Climate Changes: Adaptation and Mitigation Time Scales." Accessed June 25, 2020.

101. World Resources Institute. "4 Charts Explain Greenhouse Gas Emissions by Countries and Sectors." Accessed June 25, 2020.

102. National Oceanic and Atmospheric Administration. "NOAA's Greenhouse Gas Index Up 41 Percent Since 1990." Accessed June 25, 2020.

103. Food and Agriculture Organization of the United Nations. "Bee-ing Grateful to Our Pollinators." Accessed June 25, 2020.

104. Chicago Council on Global Affairs. "The Price of Pollinator Losses." Accessed June 25, 2020.

105. Food and Agriculture Organization of the United Nations. "The State of World Fisheries and Aquaculture," Pages 5–6. Accessed June 25, 2020.

Fixing Climate Change Through Policy Is Difficult, but Possible

United Nations Environment Programme

The United Nations Environment Programme is the branch of the UN concerned with their environmental agenda and sustainable development.

The world today laid the groundwork for a radical shift to a more sustainable future, where innovation will be harnessed to tackle environmental challenges, the use of throwaway plastics will be significantly reduced, and development will no longer cost the earth.

After five days of talks at the Fourth UN Environment Assembly in Nairobi, ministers from more than 170 United Nations Member States delivered a bold blueprint for change, saying the world needed to speed up moves towards a new model of development in order to respect the vision laid out in the Sustainable Development Goals for 2030.

Noting that they were deeply concerned by mounting evidence that the planet is increasingly polluted, rapidly warming and dangerously depleted, the ministers pledged to address environmental challenges through advancing innovative solutions and adopting sustainable consumption and production patterns.

"We reaffirm that poverty eradication, changing unsustainable and promoting sustainable patterns of consumption and production and protecting and managing the natural resource base of economic and social development are the overarching objectives of, and essential requirements for, sustainable development," the ministers said in a final declaration.

"World Pledges to Protect Polluted, Degraded Planet as It Adopts Blueprint for More Sustainable Future," United Nations Environment Programme, March 15, 2019. Reprinted by permission.

"We will improve national resource management strategies with integrated full lifecycle approaches and analysis to achieve resource-efficient and low-carbon economies," they said.

More than 4,700 delegates, including environment ministers, scientists, academics, business leaders and civil society representatives, met in Nairobi for the Assembly, the world's top environmental body whose decisions will set the global agenda, notably ahead of the UN Climate Action Summit in September.

As well as pledging to promote sustainable food systems by encouraging resilient agricultural practices, tackle poverty through sustainable management of natural resources, and promote the use and sharing of environmental data, ministers said they would significantly reduce single-use plastic products.

"We will address the damage to our ecosystems caused by the unsustainable use and disposal of plastic products, including by significantly reducing single-use plastic products by 2030, and we will work with the private sector to find affordable and environmentally friendly products," they said.

To address critical knowledge gaps, ministers promised to work towards producing comparable international environmental data while improving national monitoring systems and technologies. They also expressed support for UN Environment's efforts to develop a global environmental data strategy by 2025.

"The world is at a crossroads but today we have chosen the way forward," said Siim Kiisler, President of the Fourth UN Environment Assembly and Estonia's environment minister. "We have decided to do things differently. From reducing our dependence on single-use plastics to placing sustainability at the heart of all future development, we will transform the way we live. We have the innovative solutions we need. Now we must adopt the policies that allow us to implement them."

The Assembly started on a sombre note after the crash of an Ethiopian Airlines flight from Addis Ababa to Nairobi, which claimed the lives of all 157 people on board, including UN officials and other delegates who were travelling to the meeting. A minute's silence was held for the victims at the opening ceremony, where officials also paid tribute to their colleagues' work.

At the close of the Assembly, delegates adopted a series of non-binding resolutions, covering the logistics of shifting to a business-unusual model of development.

These included a recognition that a more circular global economy, in which goods can be reused or repurposed and kept in circulation for as long as possible, can significantly contribute to sustainable consumption and production.

Other resolutions said Member States could transform their economies through sustainable public procurement and urged countries to support measures to address food waste and develop and share best practices on energy-efficient and safe cold chain solutions.

Resolutions also addressed using incentives, including financial measures, to promote sustainable consumption while encouraging Member States to end incentives for unsustainable consumption and production where appropriate.

"Our planet has reached its limits and we need to act now. We are delighted that the world has responded here in Nairobi with firm commitments to build a future where sustainability will be the overarching objective in everything we do," said UN Environment's Acting Executive Director Joyce Msuya.

"If countries deliver on all that was agreed here and implement the resolutions, we could take a big step towards a new world order where we no longer grow at the expense of nature but instead see people and planet thrive together."

A key focus of the meeting was the need to protect oceans and fragile ecosystems. Ministers adopted a number of resolutions on marine plastic litter and microplastics, including a commitment to establish a multi-stakeholder platform within UN Environment to take immediate action towards the long-term elimination of litter and microplastics.

Another resolution called on Member States and other actors to address the problem of marine litter by looking at the full life-cycle of products and increasing resource-efficiency.

During the summit, Antigua and Barbuda, Paraguay and Trinidad and Tobago joined UN Environment's Clean Seas campaign, bringing the number of countries now involved in the world's largest alliance for combatting marine plastic pollution to 60, including 20 from Latin America and the Caribbean.

The need to act swiftly to tackle existential environmental challenges was underscored by the publication of a series of comprehensive reports during the Assembly.

Among the most devastating was an update on the changing Arctic, which found that even if the world were to cut emissions in line with the Paris Agreement, winter temperatures in the Arctic would rise 3-5°C by 2050 and 5-9°C by 2080, devastating the region and unleashing sea level rises worldwide.

A graphic look at the changing Arctic warned that rapidly thawing permafrost could even accelerate climate change further and derail efforts to meet the Paris Agreement's long-term goal of limiting the rise in global temperature to 2°C.

Meanwhile, the sixth Global Environmental Outlook, seen as the most comprehensive and rigorous assessment on the state of the planet, warned that millions of people could die prematurely from water and air pollution by 2050 unless urgent action is taken.

Produced by 250 scientists and experts from more than 70 countries, the report said the world has the science, technology and finance it needs to move towards a more sustainable development path, but politicians, business people and the public must back change.

UN Deputy Secretary-General Amina Mohammed, who attended the summit on Thursday, said action on unsustainable resource use was no longer a choice, but a necessity.

"As Member States have stated during vibrant debates, alongside civil society, businesses, the science community and other stakeholders here in Nairobi, it is yet possible to increase our well-being, and at the same time maintain economic growth through a clever mix of climate mitigation, resource efficiency and biodiversity protection policies," she said.

As evidence mounts of the devastating effects of human activity on the health of the planet, a global clamour for swift action is rising. As delegates prepared to leave Nairobi on Friday, hundreds of thousands of students in around 100 countries took to the streets as part of a global protest movement inspired by Swedish student Greta Thunberg.

Speaking during the Environment Assembly on Thursday, French President Emmanuel Macron said young people were right to protest and that the world needed their anger to drive faster, more forceful action.

"We believe that what we need, given the situation we live in, are real laws, rules that are binding and adopted internationally. Our biosphere faces total devastation. Humanity itself is threatened. We cannot simply respond with some nice-sounding principles without any real impact," President Macron said.

President Kenyatta also said that the world needed to act now to address record levels of environmental degradation, food insecurity, poverty and unemployment.

"Current global statistics are indeed quite sobering and projections for the future generations are dire and demand urgent action from governments, communities, businesses and individuals," he said.

The Green New Deal Is a Loose Framework

Danielle Kurtzleben

Danielle Kurtzleben is a political reporter for National Public Radio. She has also written for Vox *and* US News & World Report.

Whether it's a deadly cold snap or a hole under an Antarctic glacier or a terrifying new report, there seem to be constant reminders now of the dangers that climate change poses to humanity.

Rep. Alexandria Ocasio-Cortez, D-N.Y., and Sen. Ed Markey, D-Mass., think they have a start to a solution. Thursday they are introducing a framework defining what they call a "Green New Deal"—what they foresee as a massive policy package that would remake the US economy and, they hope, eliminate all US carbon emissions.

That's a really big—potentially impossibly big—undertaking.

"Even the solutions that we have considered big and bold are nowhere near the scale of the actual problem that climate change presents to us," Ocasio-Cortez told NPR's Steve Inskeep in an interview that aired Thursday on *Morning Edition*.

She added: "It could be part of a larger solution, but no one has actually scoped out what that larger solution would entail. And so that's really what we're trying to accomplish with the Green New Deal."

What Is the Green New Deal?

In very broad strokes, the Green New Deal legislation laid out by Ocasio-Cortez and Markey sets goals for some drastic measures to cut carbon emissions across the economy, from electricity generation to transportation to agriculture. In the process, it aims to create jobs and boost the economy.

"Alexandria Ocasio-Cortez Releases Green New Deal Outline," by Danielle Kurtzleben, National Public Radio Inc., February 7, 2019. Reprinted by permission.

In that vein, the proposal stresses that it aims to meet its ambitious goals while paying special attention to groups like the poor, disabled and minority communities that might be disproportionately affected by massive economic transitions like those the Green New Deal calls for.

Importantly, it's a nonbinding resolution, meaning that even if it were to pass (more on the challenges to that below), it wouldn't itself create any new programs. Instead, it would potentially affirm the sense of the House that these things should be done in the coming years.

Lawmakers pass nonbinding resolutions for things as simple as congratulating Super Bowl winners, as well as to send political messages—for example, telling the president they disapprove of his trade policies, as the Senate did in summer 2018.

What Are the Specifics of That Framework?

The bill calls for a "10-year national mobilization" toward accomplishing a series of goals that the resolution lays out.

Among the most prominent, the deal calls for "meeting 100 percent of the power demand in the United States through clean, renewable, and zero-emission energy sources." The ultimate goal is to stop using fossil fuels entirely, Ocasio-Cortez's office told NPR, as well as to transition away from nuclear energy.

In addition, the framework, as described in the legislation as well as a blog post—containing an updated version of "FAQs" provided to NPR by Ocasio-Cortez's office—calls for a variety of other lofty goals:

- "upgrading all existing buildings" in the country for energy efficiency;
- working with farmers "to eliminate pollution and greenhouse gas emissions ... as much as is technologically feasible" (while supporting family farms and promoting "universal access to healthy food");
- "Overhauling transportation systems" to reduce emissions—including expanding electric car manufacturing, building

"charging stations everywhere," and expanding high-speed rail to "a scale where air travel stops becoming necessary";

- A guaranteed job "with a family-sustaining wage, adequate family and medical leave, paid vacations and retirement security" for every American;
- "High-quality health care" for all Americans.

Which is to say: the Green New Deal framework combines big climate-change-related ideas with a wish list of progressive economic proposals that, taken together, would touch nearly every American and overhaul the economy.

Are Those Ideas Doable?

Many in the climate science community, as well as Green New Deal proponents, agree that saving the world from disastrous effects of climate change requires aggressive action.

And some of the Green New Deal's goals are indeed aggressive. For example, Ocasio-Cortez told NPR that "in 10 years, we're trying to go carbon-neutral."

According to Jesse Jenkins, a postdoctoral environmental fellow at Harvard's Kennedy School, that may be an unreachable goal.

"Where we need to be targeting really is a net-zero carbon economy by about 2050, which itself is an enormous challenge and will require reductions in carbon emissions much faster than have been achieved historically," he said. "2030 might be a little bit early to be targeting."

Similarly, removing combustible engines from the roads or expanding high-speed rail to largely eliminate air travel would require nothing short of revolutionizing transportation.

Likewise, some of the more progressive economic policies— universal health care and a job guarantee, for example—while popular among some Democrats, would also be very difficult to implement and transition into.

On top of all that, implementing all of these policies could cost trillions upon trillions of dollars.

Altogether, the Green New Deal is a loose framework. It does not lay out guidance on how to implement these policies.

Rather, the idea is that Ocasio-Cortez and Markey will "begin work immediately on Green New Deal bills to put the nuts and bolts on the plan described in this resolution."

And again, all of this is hypothetical—it would be tough to implement and potentially extremely expensive ... if it passed.

So Did the Idea of a Green New Deal Start with Ocasio-Cortez?

Not at all.

While the Green New Deal has in the last year or so grown central to progressive Democrats' policy conversations, the idea of a Green New Deal itself is well over a decade old. Environmentalists were talking about it as far back as 2003, when the term popped up in a *San Francisco Chronicle* article about an environmentalist conference.

It gained traction with a 2007 *New York Times* column from Thomas Friedman, where he used the phrase to describe the scope of energy investments he thought would be necessary to slow climate change on a large scale.

The phrase was also used around President Barack Obama's 2009 stimulus, which had around $90 billion worth of environmental initiatives.

While the idea gained some currency in Europe and also in the Green Party, it wasn't until after the 2016 election that it really gained broad popularity on the left in the US.

This latest iteration is different both in the political energy that it has amassed and the grand scope it is taking. While it was a product of the progressive activist community, Ocasio-Cortez has been perhaps the most visible proponent of the plan and has helped it gain nationwide attention.

So Will It Pass?

That looks unlikely.

Yes, there's some energy for it on the left—some House Democrats have already said they will support the bill. However, there are indications House leadership isn't prioritizing the idea as much as those more liberal Democrats would like—Speaker Nancy Pelosi frustrated Green New Deal proponents by not giving them the kind of committee they wanted to put the policies together.

After the deal's Thursday release, she also cast the plan as simply one of any number of environmental proposals the House might consider.

"It will be one of several or maybe many suggestions that we receive," Pelosi told Politico. "The green dream or whatever they call it, nobody knows what it is, but they're for it right?"

In addition, it's easy to see how the bill could be dangerous for moderate House Democrats, many of whom come from swing districts and may be loath to touch such a progressive proposal.

Among Republicans—even those worried about climate change—the package, with its liberal economic ideas, will also likely be a nonstarter.

"Someone's going to have to prove to me how that can be accomplished because it looks to me like for the foreseeable future we're gonna be using a substantial amount of fossil fuels," said Rep. Francis Rooney, R-Fla., co-chair of the bipartisan Climate Solutions Caucus, speaking to NPR before the Green New Deal's text was released.

For his part, Rooney is in favor of a carbon tax, a policy he helped propose with a bipartisan group of lawmakers in November. Information from Ocasio-Cortez's office says that the Green New Deal could include a carbon tax, but that it would be "a tiny part" of the total package of policies.

Meanwhile, there's little chance of a Green New Deal getting a vote in the Republican-controlled Senate.

If It's Not Going to Pass and It's Not Even Binding, Why Is It Worth Even Talking About?

It's worth talking about because it already is a politically powerful idea among Democrats.

Already, presidential candidates are being asked whether they support the idea of a Green New Deal, meaning it's easy to see the issue becoming a litmus test for some voters in both the 2020 congressional elections and the presidential election.

To more liberal Democrats, the prospect of such an ambitious economic and environmental package at the center of the 2020 campaign may be particularly energizing.

"I think it's like a really weird instinct that the Democratic Party develops to not be exciting intentionally," said Sean McElwee, co-founder of the progressive think tank Data for Progress. "Most of politics is getting people excited enough to show up and vote for you. And I think that a Green New Deal and Medicare-for-all—these are ideas that are big enough to get people excited and show up to vote for you."

For her part, Ocasio-Cortez says that a policy like the Green New Deal could get voters excited enough to pressure their Congress members to support it.

"I do think that when there's a wide spectrum of debate on an issue, that is where the public plays a role. That is where the public needs to call their member of Congress and say, 'This is something that I care about,'" she told NPR, adding, "Where I do have trust is in my colleagues' capacity to change and evolve and be adaptable and listen to their constituents."

That said, it's easy to see how a Green New Deal litmus test could backfire on that front, endangering some Democrats—particularly in swing districts.

But it's not just about national politics. The national-level energy for a Green New Deal could boost efforts in cities and states. New York Gov. Andrew Cuomo, for example, has been pushing a Green New Deal in his state.

Aside from the politics, there's the fact that climate change remains an impending threat—one for which the world has yet to come up with a fix.

"It's a big legislation because it's a huge [expletive] problem! We're all going to die," said McElwee. "Every week it seems like the risks of climate change become more real, and the amount of devastation it is going to wreak upon humanity becomes larger, and that means we have to do bigger things."

Nine Criticisms of the Green Economy

Barbara Unmüßig

Barbara Unmüßig is the co-president of the Heinrich Böll Foundation. She has focused on environmental issues throughout her research career.

The green economy is being put forth as a model to solve ecological and economic crises. But what are the basic assumptions of the green economy—and how are they having a practical impact?

While the Green Economy Exudes Optimism, It Is Ultimately a Matter of Faith and Selective Blind Spots

In the mainstream imagination, the green economy wants to break away from our fossil-fueled business as usual. It's a nice, optimistic message: the economy can continue to grow, and growth can be green. The green economy will even become a driver for more growth. Yet reconciling climate protection and resource conservation with economic growth in a finite and unjust world remains an illusion. With its positive associations, the term "green economy" suggests that the world as we know it can continue much as before thanks to a green growth paradigm of greater efficiency and lower resource consumption.

However, making this promise requires deliberately downplaying complexity and having powerful faith in the miracles of the market economy and technological innovation, while at the same time ignoring and not wanting to tackle existing economic and political power structures. The green economy is thus a matter of faith and selective blind spots.

"9 Theses on Criticizing the Green Economy," by Barbara Unmüßig, Green Economy Coalition, January 7, 2016. https://www.greeneconomycoalition.org/news-analysis/9 -theses-criticizing-green-economy. Licensed under CC BY-SA 4.0 International.

It can only be a realistic option for the future if it recognizes planetary boundaries and ensures the radical reduction and fair distribution of emissions and resource consumption.

Fixing the Failure of the Market by Enlarging It

Instead of rethinking business, the green economy wants to redefine nature. The green economy redefines the idea of the primacy of economics as the decisive answer to the current crises. Economics has become the currency of politics, say its advocates. Consequently, they intend to correct the failure of the market economy by enlarging the market. The green economy thus wants the market to encompass things that have previously been beyond its scope by redefining the relationship between nature and the economy.

The result is a new version of the concept of nature as natural capital and the economic services of ecosystems—and not a transformation of our way of doing business. Instead of rethinking business, the green economy wants to redefine nature by measuring and recording it, assigning it a value and putting it on the balance sheet—based on a global, abstract currency: carbon credits.

This hides the many structural causes of the environmental and climate crisis from view and no longer fully takes them into account in the search for real solutions and ways out. The consequences of such an approach are also reflected in the new market mechanisms for trading biodiversity credits. In many cases, they do not prevent the destruction of nature but merely organize it along market lines.

The green economy reduces the needed fundamental transformation to a question of economics and gives the impression that it can be implemented without major upheavals and conflicts. It does not even ask the decisive question—how to create a better future with fewer material goods, a different outlook and greater diversity.

Ecological Policy Goes Beyond Reducing Carbon Emissions

The green economy states its central decarbonization strategy in its mantra: "put a price on carbon." But this reduction to prices and a single currency unit (carbon credits) is one-dimensional.

Decarbonization can mean many things—the phasing-out of coal, oil and gas, the compensation of fossil emissions by storing equivalent quantities of carbon in plants or soils, or the use of technology for carbon capture and storage (CCS) on an industrial scale. From the social and ecological vantage points, these alternatives lead to completely different results.

The global crisis is much more than just a climate crisis. The now widely recognized system of "planetary boundaries" established by the Stockholm Resilience Centre has identified three areas where we have exceeded safe limits in the field of ecology alone:

- climate change
- loss of biodiversity
- nitrogen pollution (in particular through the use of fertilizers in agriculture)

The green economy ignores the complexities and interactive nature of these crises and reduces saving the world to the simple narrative of a business model.

Innovation as a Fetish

The green economy does not put innovation in the context of interests and power structures. Faith and trust in technological innovation is central to the promise of the green economy. But there is no doubt that we need innovation at all levels—socially, culturally and technologically—in order to realize global transformation.

Innovation, particularly of a technological nature, must always be judged in its social, cultural and environmental contexts. After all, innovation is neither automatic, nor a foregone conclusion. It is shaped by the interests and power structures of the actors. Many innovations therefore do not contribute to fundamental transformation, but legitimize the status quo and often extend the life of products and systems that are no longer fit for the future.

The automotive industry, for example, is producing more fuel-efficient engines, but also larger, more powerful and heavier vehicles than ever. At the same time, it has proven itself highly innovative in rigging emissions tests, as recently shown by the VW scandal. Furthermore, it is replacing fossil fuels with biofuels that are highly problematic, both socially and ecologically.

Can we expect such an industry to take a leading role in a transformation that will radically restructure our transportation system—to the detriment of private motor vehicles?

Innovations change our lives, but they do not work miracles. Nuclear technology did not solve the world's energy problem, nor did the green revolution end world hunger. The examples of nuclear energy, genetic engineering and geoengineering show how controversial technologies can be if their limitations and the social and ecological damage they can cause are not carefully examined in all their dimensions in advance.

The Green Economy's False Promise of Efficiency

It is true that our economy is becoming more efficient, and that is a good thing. But at the present pace, it will not be enough. For example, household appliances consume less energy, but our homes contain more electrical devices than ever before. This rebound effect reduces the impact of efficiency increases.

While a relative decoupling of growth and energy consumption is possible, we need much more in order to achieve the necessary transformation: a radical and absolute reduction of energy and resource consumption—especially in the industrialized countries. Achieving this absolute reduction is not a realistic prospect without questioning the growth-based model of prosperity.

There is no plausible scenario that credibly combines growth, an absolute reduction of environmental consumption and more global justice in a world of nine billion people.

The Green Economy Is Apolitical: It Ignores Human Rights and People Who Get Involved

The green economy has numerous blind spots: it cares little about politics, barely registers human rights, does not recognize social actors and suggests the possibility of reform without conflict. Social conflicts—such as those arising in the construction of wind farms or major dams, or in the question of who owns the carbon storage capacity of forests—are ignored.

In the wake of the realization that "business as usual" is not an option, the green economy provides a supposedly non-political vehicle to gain hegemony over the transformation path while obscuring questions of economic and political interests, power and ownership structures, human rights and the resources of power.

Realism Instead of Wishful Thinking

The future needs environmental policy that can handle conflict. To address the challenges of the future adequately, we need a realistic view of the world that is not distorted by wishful thinking. In other words, the solutions will not be simple and not everything will be "win-win." It will not always be possible to reconcile ecology and business. The required transformation will impact power interests and there will be losers. It will not be attainable without tough negotiations, conflict and resistance.

This represents a call to action for policymakers in particular. Governance has been the key to major environmental successes. Politically motivated and enforced protection of human and natural habitats is far more effective than monetizing nature and the living spaces of people who have protected their ecosystems for millennia.

Not every detail needs to be regulated, but sometimes bans on substances such as leaded gasoline, highly toxic pesticides and CFCs are indispensable, as are independent monitoring and low threshold values.

Alternatives Are Feasible

There is no lack of alternatives and good examples. Organic farming, even on a large scale, is already a reality and a highly productive sector of the economy. The theoretical underpinnings of alternative forms of networked mobility systems that do not rely primarily on private vehicles but do not rule out zero-emissions automobiles have been developed and are already being implemented in initial stages.

Above all, innovation must not be confined to the concept of technology: the development of new lifestyles and new forms of urban life also constitute innovation. A decentralized and renewable energy supply is within the reach of realpolitik, as is the elimination of environmentally harmful subsidies.

So for the most part there is no shortage of alternatives, but a lack of power to implement them, especially against the resistance of entrenched minority interests. For such a perspective, a fixation on the question of "how can we achieve green growth?" is counterproductive.

The Question of Power: For a Re-Politicization of Environmental Policy

Radical realism is central to an understanding of political ecology that does not shrink back from uncomfortable questions and that seeks majorities in society for a socially and ecologically just transformation. The authors call for a re-politicization of environmental policy and a return to the term "political ecology" as a way of understanding the complex relationships between politics and ecology and between humans and nature, and to give environmental policy and control precedence over economic interests.

Social, cultural and technological innovation must become more closely intertwined. Technologies—and especially their social and ecological impact—must be subject to wide debate and democratic control.

A greening of the economy through resource conservation, the transition to renewable energies, better technology and effective economic incentives such as taxes is undeniably a part of the solution.

However, the project of a global socio-ecological transformation goes much further: It must question established power, prioritize democratically legitimated decision-making processes and structures, and focus on compliance with fundamental environmental and human rights.

The trend reversal will need to be more radical than the green economy's proposals. It will not be possible without passion and optimism, and not without controversy and struggle. The book *Kritik der Grünen Ökonomie* sees itself as a part of the global search and an invitation to the debate.

Green Growth Won't Save the Planet

Oliver Taherzadeh and Benedict Probst

Oliver Taherzadeh is a PhD researcher in the Department of Geography at the University of Cambridge. Benedict Probst is a PhD researcher at Cambridge Centre for Environment, Energy and Natural Resource Governance at the University of Cambridge.

Green growth has emerged as the dominant narrative for tackling contemporary environmental problems. Its supporters, including the likes of the UN, OECD, national governments, businesses and even NGOs, say that sustainability can be achieved through efficiency, technology and market-led environmental action. Green growth suggests we really can have our cake and eat it—both growing the economy and protecting the planet.

But when it comes to tackling the most pressing environmental problems such as climate breakdown, species extinction or resource depletion, green growth might weaken rather than strengthen progress. Here are five reasons why:

1. Growth Trumps Efficiency

In theory, advances in environmental efficiency can help to "decouple" economic growth from resource use and pollution. But such outcomes remain elusive in the real world. While sectors such as construction, agriculture and transport have managed to create less pollution and use less resources per unit of output, these improvements have struggled to fully offset the scale and speed of economic growth. By outpacing production improvements, economic growth has led to an unhampered rise in resource use, pollution, and waste.

In fact, efficiency may even be fuelling further consumption and pollution. This is a paradox first observed in 1865 by the economist William Stanley Jevons, who noticed the introduction of a more efficient steam engine actually coincided with more coal consumption, not less, as new profits were reinvested in extra production, causing prices to fall, demand to rise, and so on. Such "rebound effects" exist across the whole economy, so the only real solution is to consume less. At best, efficiency is a half-baked solution, at worst, it stokes the very problem it tries to address.

2. Overstated Technology

Proponents of green growth want us to believe that ever better technology is the solution. However, we are not so sure. International environmental agreements and scenarios confidently assume large scale technologies will be deployed to capture and store carbon emissions, but we have yet to witness their potential even on a small scale. Mechanised agriculture is being promoted on the basis of increased efficiency and yield while overlooking the fact that low-tech farming is a more productive means of meeting global food demand at lower environmental cost.

Clearly, technology is crucial in lowering the environmental burden of production and consumption, but green growth overstates its role.

3. No Profit, No Action

Perhaps the most compelling argument put forward for green growth is that protecting the environment can go hand-in-hand with making profits. However, in reality there is often a tension between these goals. Many firms are risk averse, for instance, and don't want to be first-movers, whether on charging for plastic bags, banning plastic cups or introducing carbon labelling.

Then you have the fact that some sustainable interventions are simply not attractive investments for the private sector: there is little profit to be made in conserving ecosystems or financing public infrastructure for electric vehicles. Meanwhile, environmental risks like natural resource depletion or extreme weather might become increasingly attractive to part of the private sector.

If we're serious about living within environmental limits we need to say adios to certain sectors: fossil fuels, livestock and fertilisers. If we leave that to the market, we're going to be waiting a long, long time.

4. Green Consumption Is Still Consumption

Buying "green" offers a seemingly common sense solution to the environmental ills of over-consumption, but we're sceptical. The push for greener consumption has devolved responsibility from governments and business to ordinary people. As one commentator put it, we have been conned into fighting environmental issues as individuals, while the real culprits get off scot-free.

Indeed, the very act of green consumption still fuels the extraction and use of natural resources, pollution and environmental degradation. Stuff requires more stuff to produce—this is often overlooked when we buy re-useable cups, eco-appliances and "sustainable" clothing. Any positive impacts of green consumption can also easily be undone through people feeling they have a moral license to indulge elsewhere. Green consumption is a zero sum game if we decide to go vegan then fly long haul. While it's misguided to think consumers can't make a difference, we shouldn't be fooled into thinking humanity can consume its way out of environmental problems.

5. The Danger of Guesswork

A central principle of green growth is that markets are both part of the problem and solution. Proponents of green growth argue that as long as we get the numbers right—a tax on carbon, a clean energy subsidy, or a price tag on nature—markets can foster sustainability. But tackling environmental problems through the market involves a lot of guesswork with no guaranteed outcome.

Unlike carbon, ecosystems and biodiversity are not amenable to economic valuation and substitution within markets. Pricing environmental damage in markets is like selling permits to pollute and trash our natural world. Although market mechanisms can guide business towards sustainable behaviour, only stringent laws and regulation can help bring their growth in line with environmental limits.

Beyond Green Growth?

Efficiency alone is a blunt tool and techno-fixes will also not get us where we need to be. We need to address the elephant in the room: consumption. As the business case for reducing consumption is poor, governments and communities need to take charge.

There are promising signs. The next major Intergovernmental Panel on Climate Change (IPCC) assessment report will finally include a chapter on tackling consumption. In the UK, the Committee on Climate Change's report on net zero by 2050 highlights the critical need for societal change. Questioning our appetite for growth is the first step towards a more inclusive and effective model for sustainability.

The Green Growth Myth

Christine Corlet Walker

Christine Corlet Walker is a PhD candidate at the University of Surrey. Her research focuses on balancing a high quality of life with the health of the planet.

You may have missed it, but a recent report declared that the main strategy of world leaders for tackling climate change won't work. It's called green growth, and it's favoured by some of the largest and most influential organisations in the world, including the United Nations and the World Bank.

Green growth is a vague term with many definitions, but broadly speaking, it's the idea that society can reduce its environmental impacts and slash its emissions, even while the economy continues to grow and the quantity of stuff that's produced and consumed increases.

This would be achieved by improving the efficiency of production and manufacturing processes, transitioning to cleaner energy sources and developing new technologies to deal with the pollution that economic activity creates. Better yet, it's argued, all of this could be done fast enough to meet the Paris Agreement target of keeping global warming to below 1.5°C.

Fixing the climate crisis without having to compromise on economic growth sounds appealing. But the Decoupling Debunked report echoes work by prominent academics in finding that there is no evidence that societies have ever managed to decouple economic growth from emissions at this scale in the past, and little evidence they have the capacity to achieve it in the future.

It's no surprise that, historically, global carbon emissions have gone up as economies have grown. The processes that produce the

"Green Growth Is Trusted to Fix Climate Change—Here's the Problem with That," by Christine Corlet Walker, The Conversation, August 5, 2019. https://theconversation.com /green-growth-is-trusted-to-fix-climate-change-heres-the-problem-with-that-120785. Licensed under CC BY-ND 4.0 International.

goods and services we all consume use raw materials as inputs and generate pollution, carbon emissions and waste.

Making these processes more efficient and swapping fossil fuels for renewables can, and has, reduced the average emissions that come with each additional dollar of economic growth. This is known as "relative decoupling," because each dollar of new economic growth has fewer emissions attached to it, relative to each dollar of past growth. But, emissions still rise in absolute terms because the economy is still growing.

Since it is the total amount of carbon in the atmosphere that matters in the race against climate change, we need to contrast this idea of "relative decoupling" with the stronger concept of "absolute decoupling." Absolute decoupling means that even as the economy grows, total carbon emissions fall year-on-year.

With this distinction in mind, the question becomes: is absolute decoupling of economic growth from carbon emissions possible? And can it be done fast enough to prevent catastrophic climate change?

The Scale of the Challenge

According to the IPCC, there is a 66% likelihood that the world can remain under the Paris Agreement target of 1.5°C of warming if we emit no more than 420 billion additional tonnes of carbon into the atmosphere, from early 2018.

Humans currently emit about 37 billion tonnes of carbon every year, and that number is still growing. Even the most generous projections suggest that if emissions continue at this rate, the carbon budget will be used up in less than 20 years.

The rate of decarbonisation that's needed is huge, and far in excess of anything that's been seen previously. Economic growth makes that challenge even harder, as gains in decarbonisation may be outweighed by increases in production and consumption. But green growth advocates insist it's possible.

The IPCC's Special Report, released in October 2018, gives 90 scenarios that would be consistent with limiting warming to

1.5°C, while also continuing with economic growth. So far, so good. But almost every single one of these scenarios relies on a negative emissions technology called Bioenergy Carbon Capture and Storage (BECCS) that's completely untested at large scales.

BECCS involves growing large plantations of trees, which draw down carbon from the atmosphere, then harvesting and burning them to generate energy. The CO_2 emissions from this process are then stored underground. To limit warming to 1.5°C, this technology would need to absorb 3–7 billion tonnes of carbon from the atmosphere every year. That's at least 2,000 times more than it's currently capable of doing.

In order to absorb that much carbon, an area two to three times the size of India would need to be covered with tree plantations. Think about the difficulty of acquiring that much land, the pressure it would put on other land uses, like food production, and how much natural habitat it could erase.

No one can say that these feats are categorically impossible. But the evidence suggests that the chances of meeting the 1.5°C warming target alongside continued economic growth are, at best, highly unlikely. Can we really take this risk—relying on unproven technologies to rescue us from the threat of climate change? Given the consequences of getting the gamble wrong, surely the answer is no.

Where Does This Leave Us?

Proposals for green growth that rely solely on technology to solve the climate crisis are based on a flawed idea. This is, that the limits to the world's physical systems are flexible, but the structure of its economies are not. This seems entirely backwards and more a reflection of the importance of politics and power in determining what solutions are deemed viable, than any reflection of reality.

So society should ask, are these global institutions promoting green growth because they believe it's the most promising way of avoiding climate breakdown? Or is it because they believe it's simply not politically feasible to talk about the alternatives?

If we can be optimistic about humanity's ability to develop fantastical new technologies to bend and overcome the limits of nature, can't we lend that same optimism to developing new economic structures? Our goal in the 21st century should be creating economies that allow people to flourish, even when they don't grow.

Chapter 4

Is a Green Economy Financially and Politically Feasible?

Overview: Green Growth or No Growth

Alex Bowen

Alex Bowen is a special adviser at the Grantham Research Institute at the London School of Economics.

The current climate emergency is at last getting more of the attention it deserves, thanks to the Extinction Rebellion demonstrations and the success of Green parties in last month's European Parliament elections. But how should economic policymakers react? Should they be concentrating on making growth green—adopting the new "green growth" paradigm—or seeking prosperity without growth?

Many international economic organisations, including the Organisation for Economic Co-operation and Development, International Monetary Fund and World Bank, have been advocating the former. There is even a treaty-based, intergovernmental Global Green Growth Institute, "dedicated to supporting and promoting strong, inclusive and sustainable economic growth in developing countries and emerging economies." On the climate change front, Nicholas Stern has made a strong case that a "committed and strong low-carbon transition could trigger a new wave of economic and technological transformation and investment, a new era of global and sustainable prosperity" and the New Climate Economy project has laid out a route map towards "better growth, better climate."

Yet there is a strong current of opinion that views this pro-growth approach as fundamentally wrong-headed, on theoretical and empirical grounds. This line of thought can be traced back through the debates about the Club of Rome's 1972 report, The Limits to Growth, all the way to Thomas Malthus and John Stuart Mill.

"Green Growth or No Growth," by Alex Bowen, Grantham Research Institute on Climate Change and the Environment at the London School of Economics and Political Science, June 4, 2019. Reprinted by permission.

Give Green Growth a Chance

I reckon that green growth ought to be given a chance. The switch from our current global economic trajectory requires a huge, pervasive and persistent effort of collective action. That is more likely to happen if people and politicians see something in the switch for them. The evidence suggests that economic growth does tend to promote reported human happiness and—perhaps more relevant for policymakers—tends to help politicians win votes. Economic growth has helped to lift millions out of poverty and save lives.

But is continued economic growth possible even if it is desirable? I take some comfort from the fact that estimates of the costs of stopping human-induced climate change—the "greatest market failure the world has seen" (Nicholas Stern's words again)—are relatively modest. Aiming to keep the increase in global temperature from pre-industrial times below 1.5°C would probably only knock 0.1 percentage points off the average annual growth rate of GDP over the 21st century. But that is no reason for complacency. So far, the global community has not stepped up to meet this modest cost.

And there are many other intractable environmental problems, several of which are serious global risks, that are a lot less well understood than global warming and less amenable to mitigation by economic policy tools. But that points to the need for further study, evaluation and straight talk by politicians willing to take the long view. If collective action in response to this challenge is politically infeasible, I certainly do not rate highly the chances of persuading politicians to go for "no growth" instead.

I understand the pessimism of those who look at the track record so far of efforts to decouple economic growth from environmental degradation and material scarcity. Hickel and Kallis recently argued that "there is no empirical evidence that absolute decoupling from resource use can be achieved on a global scale against a background of continued economic growth." They are highly sceptical about economic projections based on increases in the efficiency with which raw materials are used and highlight the danger of rich countries offloading environmentally harmful and profligate activities to low-income countries. Some of their concerns are echoed by advocates of green growth such as the OECD.

But looking at the historical record over a period when policymakers have not prioritised efficient use of natural resources misleads us about what could be done in the future. Indeed, so far, governments have instead been subsidising resource exploitation. Perhaps around US$1 trillion is spent on directly subsidising the consumption of resources, including approximately $400 billion on energy, $200–300 billion of equivalent support on agriculture, and $200–300 billion on water. The authors who made this observation also note that, "While these direct subsidies are vast, they pale in comparison with the indirect subsidies in the form of natural assets that governments have failed to properly price. There is another US$1 trillion, very approximately, in the form of subsidy for the use of the atmosphere as a sink for greenhouse gas emissions. The indirect subsidy associated with lack of payments for biodiversity loss and other environmental costs is estimated at perhaps as much as $6.6 trillion."

Yet with the right price signals and regulatory contexts—and, of course, technological advances—resource productivity can increase dramatically, as we have seen with, for example, silicon chips and LED lighting. Progress (though not yet enough) is being made by some countries, including the UK, in decoupling economic growth from the growth in carbon emissions. Much more needs to be done to price raw materials and environmental capital properly, and to spread advances in materials productivity around the world, especially to the newly industrialising nations of the Global South.

Less "Stuff," More "Human Intelligence"

The most important way of decoupling natural resource use and environmental harm from economic growth is to change the nature of economic growth. Much more emphasis needs to be put on the generation and use of ideas rather than the exploitation of nature. As Baptist and Hepburn have argued, treading lightly on the planet need not reduce economic growth in value terms. They found that, in the US, sectors with lower material intensity had higher total factor productivity, as did those with higher labour intensity. In other words, using less "stuff" and more "human intelligence" increased overall productivity and economic output.

The "weightless" economy discussed by Danny Quah and Diane Coyle may be able to escape the confines of resource scarcity by exploiting the infinite expansibility of the global knowledge base. Like the fight against climate change, this will require collective action on a massive scale, for example to regulate the owners of the intellectual property that is potentially so valuable. That seems a worthwhile challenge to me—and, despite its difficulties—an easier one to meet than persuading people to give up on growth.

Eight Ideas to Limit the Fossil Fuel Industry

Fiona Harvey, Damian Carrington, Jonathan Watts,
and Patrick Greenfield

Fiona Harvey and Patrick Greenfield are environmental journalists.
Damian Carrington and Jonathan Watts are environment editors
at the Guardian.

I ndividual actions, such as flying less or buying electric cars, are helpful, but they will be futile without collective political action to slash emissions on a corporate, national and global scale. Politicians need to feel this is a priority for the electorate. That means keeping the subject high on the agenda for MPs with questions, protests, emails, social media posts, lobbying by NGOs and most of all through voting choices. Politicians need to know the public is behind them if they are to take on the petrochemical industry.

End Fossil Fuel Subsidies

The coal, oil and gas industries benefit from $5tn dollars a year—$10m a minute—according to the International Monetary Fund, which described its own estimate as "shocking." Even direct consumption subsidies for fossil fuels are double those for renewables, which the International Energy Agency says "greatly complicates the task" of tackling the climate crisis. The biggest subsidisers, the G20 nations, pledged in 2009 to end the handouts, but progress has been very limited. The UN secretary general, António Guterres, attacked the incentives in May, saying: "What we are doing is using taxpayers' money ... to destroy the world." Any change has to include provisions for social justice. Cuts in fuel subsidies should not be used as an austerity measure that hurts the poor most.

"How Do We Rein in the Fossil Fuel Industry? Here Are Eight Ideas," by Fiona Harvey, Damian Carrington, Jonathan Watts, and Patrick Greenfield, Guardian News and Media Limited, October 14, 2019. Reprinted by permission.

Put a Price on Carbon

The idea of putting a price on carbon has been around since the early 1990s and a cap-and-trade system was incorporated into the 1997 Kyoto protocol. Under cap-and-trade, a limit is set on emissions and businesses issued with permits to emit carbon. Those cutting their emissions fastest can sell spare permits to laggards, while the cap is ratcheted down over time. But success depends on a strict cap and a scarcity of permits, and the EU's scheme has been widely criticised. An alternative is a tax, which forces companies to factor the damage caused by climate change into their business decisions, and should encourage them to cut waste, cut emissions and use clean technology. The danger is of carbon leakage: that the extra cost in one country might encourage businesses to look elsewhere to site their factories. This can be dealt with by a border adjustment tax, as the EU's new commissioner pledged this week. Carbon taxes don't have to create economic losers, either—revenue neutral taxes redistribute the money to the people and are advocated by many.

Scale Back Demand for Fossil Fuels

Oil companies will sell oil for as long as there are buyers. Public shaming and social and political pressure can work to force companies to own up to their activities but most oil and gas around the world is produced by national oil companies, and they need no social licence to operate beyond that granted by their governments, which are often autocratic or unresponsive to public opinion. All companies are responsive to economic pressure, however. The only way to cut emissions from oil in the long term is to stop using oil. Reducing demand is driven by government regulation and by technological development (also driven by regulation), such as cheaper solar panels, offshore windfarms, electric cars and improved public transport.

Stop Flaring

If oil and gas are to be extracted, the least oil companies can do is extract efficiently. The World Bank has estimated that the amount of gas wastefully flared globally each year, if used for power generation instead, could supply all of Africa's electricity needs. The FT reported earlier this year that flaring in Texas was lighting up the night sky as producers let off the gas to get the oil to market quickly, to turn a faster buck regardless of the environmental consequences. The World Bank wants an end to routine flaring globally by 2030—yet in 2018 it increased.

Roll Out Large Scale Carbon Capture and Storage

Trapping and burying the CO_2 from fossil fuel burning is possible but not yet deployed at scale. Without this, the Intergovernmental Panel on Climate Change says tackling the climate crisis will be much more expensive. Oil companies have the expertise to roll out CCS but say that without a price on carbon emissions there is no commercial incentive. CCS could be used to actually remove CO_2 from the atmosphere by growing trees and plants, burning them for electricity, then sequestering the emissions. But the IPCC has warned that doing this at large scale could conflict with growing food.

Halt Investment in Fossil Fuels

The energy transition poses many risks and opportunities for investors, but it cannot be that well-intentioned savers seeking to use their money to support renewable energy businesses and divest from fossil fuels are still inadvertently investing in oil, gas and coal companies. Green investing must be regulated to ensure it really is green.

Establish Market Metrics on Climate Change

Nearly three years after the Paris agreement, world markets still have no mandatory, comparable data to measure the risks posed by the climate crisis at a company level. Regulators must act urgently—slow-moving voluntary schemes are not enough. Last week, the governor of the Bank of England warned major corporations that they had two years to agree on rules for reporting climate risks before global regulators devised their own and made them compulsory. If markets do not understand what climate change really means for car manufacturers, fossil fuel companies and energy firms, a climate-induced financial crisis is just a matter of time. Investment in fossil fuels must end. The fossil fuel divestment movement now has $11.5tn of assets under management committed to divestment.

Money Should Be Created to Support Green Investment

Paul De Grauwe

Paul De Grauwe is the John Paulson Chair of European Political Economy at the London School of Economics' European Institute.

To what extent can the money created by the central bank be used to finance investments in the environment? This is a question that is often asked today. The green activists respond with enthusiasm that the central bank, and in particular the European Central Bank (ECB), should act and stimulate the financing of environmental investments through the printing of money. The ECB has created 2,600 billion euros of new money since 2015 in the context of its quantitative easing (QE) program. All that money has gone to financial institutions that have done very little with it. Why can't the ECB inject the money into environmental investments instead of pouring it into the financial sector?

Most traditional economists react with horror. The ECB should not interfere with the environment, they say. The government should do that. If the ECB jumps on the environmental bandwagon, it will be obliged to print too much money. This will fuel inflation in the long run, with terrible consequences. Ultimately, the environment will not be served.

Who is right in this debate? To answer that question, it is good to recall the basics of money creation by the ECB (or any modern central bank). Money is created by the ECB when that institution buys financial assets in the market. The suppliers of these assets are financial institutions. These then obtain a deposit in euros at the ECB in exchange for relinquishing these financial assets. That is the moment when money is created. This money (deposits)

"Green Money Without Inflation," by Paul De Grauwe, Council on Economic Policies, March 7, 2019. Reprinted by permission.

can then be used by the financial institutions to extend loans to companies and households.

There is no limit to the amount of financial assets that the ECB can buy. In principle, the ECB could purchase all existing financial assets (all bonds and shares, for example), but that would increase the money supply in such a way that inflation would increase dramatically. In other words, the value of the money issued by the ECB would fall sharply. To avoid this, the ECB has set a limit: it promises not to let inflation rise above 2%. That imposes a constraint on the amount of money that the ECB can create. So far, the ECB has been successful in maintaining the 2% inflation target.

There is also no restriction on what types of assets the ECB can buy. Since 2015 when it started its QE-program, the ECB has mainly bought government bonds, but also corporate bonds from financial institutions. The ECB could, however, also purchase bonds issued to finance environmental investments. The only restriction on these purchases (again) is that they do not endanger the 2% inflation target.

What are the options for the ECB? The ECB has bought 2,600 billion of government and corporate bonds since 2015. These purchases have not fueled inflation, which has remained below 2% in the Eurozone. The ECB has now stopped making new purchases. It has announced though that when these government and corporate bonds come to maturity, new bonds will be bought in the market so as to keep the money stock (money base) unchanged. This creates a "window of opportunities" for the ECB. It could replace the old bonds with new "environmental bonds," i.e. bonds that have been issued to finance environmental projects. In doing so, the ECB would not create new money. It would only reorient money flows towards environmental projects. As the total amount of money would remain the same there would be no risk of additional inflation.

A possible objection is the following. If the ECB buys these "environmental bonds," it will be involved in the decision-making process about which environmental investments should have a priority. For example it would have to answer questions such as: How much public and private investments must be made? Should it be renewable energy or nuclear energy? Should the priority be given to public transport? These are all questions that have to be settled by political authorities, and not by the central bank.

One possible way out: The European authorities give a mandate to the European Investment Bank (EIB) to finance, for example, 1000 billion of environmental investments. These political authorities add guidelines for the EIB about environmental priorities. The EIB issues bonds to obtain the resources necessary to fund these investments. This is the moment the ECB can step in by buying the EIB-bonds at a pace dictated by the expiration of the old bonds on its balance sheet. This way the ECB creates "green money" without fueling inflation. At the same time, as the ECB buys EIB bonds, it creates the possibility for the EIB to increase its borrowing in the capital markets without endangering its AAA-status.

The bottom line is that it is perfectly possible for the ECB to use the instrument of money creation to favour environmental investments without endangering price stability. Of course, one could also argue that the ECB could use its monetary instrument to favour other worthwhile projects, e.g. poverty reduction. This is certainly true, and if a majority of the population were to desire this, it should be done. Nevertheless, I am rather reluctant to go in this direction, as it would create the risk that the ECB is loaded with too many social responsibilities that it cannot handle properly.

That's why I conclude that given the existential nature of the degradation of the environment, including climate change, the priority should be to use the ECB's money creation capacity towards the support of environmental projects. This can be done without creating inflation.

Politicians Must Mine the Divide Between Coal Lobbies and Energy Companies

Christian Downie

Christian Downie is an Australian Research Council DECRA Fellow in the School of Regulation and Global Governance at the Australian National University.

I t's time we started talking about the principal opponents to action on climate change—fossil fuel industries. If history has taught us anything, it is when oil, gas and coal industries oppose policies to reduce greenhouse gas emissions, those policies fail.

And make no mistake, they do oppose. Revelations this year that mining giant Glencore spent millions of dollars globally to bankroll a pro-coal campaign are just the latest example.

However, my research shows that there are specific strategies policymakers can use to help overcome the resistance from incumbent fossil fuel industries, including exploiting the divisions within and between fossil fuel industries.

I have spent the past few years studying the behaviour of these firms and industries in the United States—the home of fossil fuel resistance. After all, the US is now the largest producer of oil and gas, with the largest reserves of coal on the planet, and it is the home of companies, such as ExxonMobil, that have known about climate change for 40 years and have been denying its existence for almost as long.

To get to know the way they work, I spent countless hours in the offices of major coal corporations and their lobbyists. I met with executives from oil and gas corporations in Houston, and their lobbyists in Washington DC.

"Politicians Must Mine the Divide Between Coal Lobbies and Energy Companies," by Christian Downie, The Conversation, October 23, 2019. https://theconversation.com /politicians-must-mine-the-divide-between-coal-lobbies-and-energy-companies-124877. Licensed under CC BY-ND 4.0 International.

I also spoke with small renewable startups, and billion-dollar companies running endless battles to preserve tax subsidies for wind and solar, which they claimed were only fair given the subsidies to fossil fuels.

So what are the lessons for policymakers seeking to advance a clean energy transition? Three stand out.

Support Clean Energy Industries

First, governments need to entrench and build existing interests in support of clean energy. Targeted policies, such as subsidies to the solar industry or tax rebates to households for solar power, both boost the industry and build a specific political constituency in support of solar power.

For example, US investment tax credits for solar power helped drive a boom in recent years, growing into an industry measured in the billions of dollars. As industry revenues increased, so has the industry's power to defend the investment tax credit and oppose fossil fuel companies.

Indeed, the Solar Energy Industries Association in the US is now a vocal advocate for clean energy in Washington, just as the Solar Council is here in Australia. Both groups have helped offset the tide of fossil fuel lobbying that regularly washes against the shores of government.

Split Fossil Fuel Industries

Second, policymakers should seek to exploit divisions within and between fossil fuel industries. When incumbent industries are divided or politically weak, green coalitions are easier to build.

For example, if the aim is to regulate coal, policies are more likely to succeed if they exploit the natural divisions between coal mining companies and the electric utilities that burn it to generate electricity.

In this case, the best bet is to target politically weak industries less able to mount a resistance campaign.

In the US the obvious example is the coal industry. The US coal industry is in structural decline, with production and revenue falling steadily. In fact, between 2012 and 2015, more than 50 firms representing 50% of US coal production filed for bankruptcy protection, including three of the largest: Peabody Energy, Alpha Natural Resources, and Arch Coal, all of whose share prices have plummeted.

Coal's decline has been manifest in a shrinking lobbying presence, with key coalitions reducing their operations, and with it the industry's capacity to oppose policies that support clean energy.

Shift Interests

Third, policymakers should not only seek to entrench existing commercial interests and exploit divisions, but also to shift commercial interests.

Policies, such as renewable energy targets that compel utilities to invest in renewable energy, over time will shift the commercial interests of these firms towards policies supporting renewable energy.

Indeed, repeat signals demonstrating to business the regulatory landscape is changing can create a tipping point, when a critical mass of affected companies stop opposing a specific policy such as emissions trading.

This was the view of many electric utilities during the Obama administration who decided to support climate policies. As the CEO of Duke Energy, Jim Rogers put it at the time, "if you're not at the table, you're going to be on the menu."

Of course none of this will be easy. BHP shareholders last week voted to remain a member of the coal lobby Minerals Council of Australia, showing the fossil fuel industries are far from toothless.

But with the science showing a third of the world's oil reserves, half the world's gas reserves and 90% of global coal reserves must be left in the ground to meet the Paris targets, governments urgently need effective action.

Otherwise, no matter what administration is in power, climate action will continue to be delayed, and even derailed by the industries that stand to lose.

We Can't Seem to Quit Fossil Fuels

Duncan Clark

Duncan Clark is a writer, researcher, and co-founder of the digital journalism company Kiln.

We have far more oil, coal and gas than we can safely burn. For all the millions of words written about climate change, the challenge really comes down to this: fuel is enormously useful, massively valuable and hugely important geopolitically, but tackling global warming means leaving most of it in the ground—by choice. Although we often hear more about green technology, consumption levels or population growth, leaving fuel in the ground is the crux of the issue. After all, the climate doesn't know or care how much renewable or nuclear energy we've got, how efficient our cars and homes are, how many people there are, or even how we run the economy. It only cares how much globe-warming pollution we emit—and that may be curiously immune to the measures we usually assume will help.

There are three facts that tell you all you really need to know about climate science and politics. One: for all the uncertainty about the detail, every science academy in the world accepts the mainstream view of man-made global warming. Two: virtually every government, recognising the profound danger of tampering with the climate that allowed human society to thrive, has agreed the world must limit the global temperature increase to 2C—a level which isn't by any means "safe" but may be enough to avoid the worst impacts. Three: the amount of warming we will experience goes up roughly in proportion to the total amount of carbon that global society emits—cumulatively.

Here is the rub. Even if we gave up on all the obscure and unconventional fossil fuel resources that companies are spending

"Why Can't We Quit Fossil Fuels?" by Duncan Clark, Guardian News and Media Limited, April 17, 2013. Reprinted by permission.

billions trying to access and just burned the "proven" oil, coal and gas reserves—the ones that are already economically viable—we would emit almost 3tn tonnes of carbon dioxide. No one can say exactly how much warming that would cause, but it is overwhelmingly likely that we would shoot well past 2C and towards 3C or even 4C of warming.

Four degrees might not sound much but at the planetary level it is. It is about the same as the temperature increase observed since the ice age's "last glacial maximum," when much of the northern hemisphere was trapped under ice as thick as the world's five tallest skyscrapers stacked on top of each other. It is impossible to say what changes another three or four degrees would bring, but the impacts could very plausibly include a collapse in global food production, catastrophic droughts and floods, heatwaves and the beginning of ice-sheet melt that could eventually raise the sea level enough to wipe out many of the world's great cities.

Sceptics argue that this doomsday scenario might not come to pass—and they are right. If we are lucky, the impact of burning all that oil, coal and gas could turn out to be at the less severe end of the plausible spectrum. But that is hardly reassuring: it's akin to saying that it is fine to walk blindfolded into a main road since you can't be sure there are any cars coming. After less than 1C of temperature increase so far, we are already seeing some profound changes, including a collapse in Arctic sea ice coverage more severe than even the most pessimistic predictions from just a few years ago. (Brits secretly hoping for a hotter future, be warned: that collapsing sea ice may have caused the freakish jet stream behaviour that made 2012 the wettest English year on record and obliterated this year's spring, both mere amuse-bouche for the feast of climate impacts expected in coming decades, even from the carbon we've emitted so far.)

Given what is at stake, it is no wonder that governments agree global warming must be stopped. But that is where the common sense ends and the cognitive dissonance begins. Because to have a decent chance of not exceeding the already risky global target, we need to start phasing out fossil fuels now at a fast enough rate to bring down emissions globally by a few percent a year, and continue doing so for decades to come.

Now compare that with what is actually happening. As with the climate, to understand the situation properly it is necessary to zoom right out to see the long-term trend. Doing so reveals something fascinating, worrying and oddly overlooked. As scientists from Lancaster University pointed out last year, if you plot a graph showing all the carbon emissions that humans have pumped into the air, the result is a remarkably clear exponential curve stretching all the way back to the mid-19th century. Zoom back in on the past decade and it is clear that for all the mounting scientific concern, the political rhetoric and the clean technology, nothing has made a jot of difference to the long-term trend at the global level—the system level. The growth rate in total carbon emissions in the past decade, at around 2% a year, was the same as that of the 1850s.

That might sound hard to believe. After all, thanks to green policies and technologies, emissions have been falling in Europe, the US and many other countries. Wind turbines and solar panels are ever-more common, not just in the west but in fast-growing China. And the energy efficiency of cars, light bulbs, homes and whole economies has been improving globally for decades. So why isn't the carbon curve showing any let up? Some might instinctively want to blame the growing population but that doesn't stack up. The rate of population growth has dropped like a stone since the 1960s and is no longer exponential, but the carbon curve doesn't appear to have noticed that any more than it has noticed the Kyoto protocol or whether you cycled to work this morning. For whatever reason, cutting carbon has so far been like squeezing a balloon: gains made in one place have been cancelled out by increases elsewhere.

To understand what is going wrong, it is necessary to consider the nature of exponential growth. This type of accelerating trend crops up when there is a feedback loop at work. For example, a credit card debt grows exponentially because interest gets applied to ever more interest. The number of algae in a jar grows in the same way: as long as there is food and air, there will be more algae and so they can breed faster.The fact that our carbon emissions have followed the same accelerating trend suggests that our use of energy is driven by a similar kind of feedback loop which is cancelling out apparent green gains.

That certainly fits with history. The industrial revolution that kick-started the human impact on the climate was driven by just such a feedback. The steam engine enabled us to drain coal mines, providing access to more coal that could power more steam engines capable of extracting yet more coal. That led to better technologies and materials that eventually helped ramp up production of oil as well. But oil didn't displace coal, it helped us mine it more effectively and stimulated more technologies that raised energy demand overall. So coal use kept rising too—and oil use in turn kept increasing as cleaner gas, nuclear and hydro came on stream, helping power the digital age, which unlocked more advanced technologies capable of opening up harder-to-read fossil-fuel reserves.

Seen as a technology-driven feedback loop, it is not surprising that nothing has yet tamed the global emissions curve, because so far nothing has cut off its food supply: fossil fuels. Indeed, though our governments now subsidise clean-power sources and efficient cars and buildings—and encourage us all to use less energy—they are continuing to undermine all that by ripping as much oil, coal and gas out of the ground as possible. And if their own green policies mean there isn't a market for these fuels at home, then no matter: they can just be exported instead.

This extraordinary double-think is everywhere to be seen. Take the US. Obama boasts that American emissions are now falling due to rising auto efficiency standards and gas displacing dirtier coal in the energy mix. But the US is extracting carbon and flowing it into the global energy system faster than ever before. Its gas boom has simply allowed it to export more of the coal to other countries such as China—which of course uses it partly to produce goods for US markets. Not happy with increasing US carbon extraction, Obama is also set to approve the Keystone XL Pipeline that will enable Canada to flood the global markets with crude produced from dirty tar sands. So much for carbon cuts.

Or take Australia, which in the same year introduced a carbon tax and started debating plans for a series of "mega-mines" that would massively increase its coal exports, helping build confidence among the companies and governments planning no fewer than 1,200 new coal-fired power stations around the world. Even the UK, with its world-leading carbon targets, gives tax-breaks to encourage oil and gas recovery and has been growing its total carbon footprint by relying ever more on Chinese factories—and therefore indirectly its reliance on American and Australian coal. And not just that. Although it rarely gets commented on, Britain—along with other supposedly green nations such as Germany—regularly begs Saudi Arabia and the other Opec nations to produce not less oil, but more. As journalist George Monbiot once put it, nations are trying simultaneously to "reduce demand for fossil fuels and increase supply."

It is not just governments that are in near-universal denial about what needs to happen to the fossil fuel sector. Blithely ignoring the fact that there is already far more accessible fuel than can be safely burned, pension fund managers and other investors are allowing listed fossil fuel companies to spend the best part of $1tn a year (comparable to the US defence budget, or more than $100 for every person on the planet) to find and develop yet more reserves.

If and when we emerge from this insanity, the carbon bubble will burst and those investments will turn out to have been as toxic as sub-prime mortgages. Don't take my word for it. HSBC analysts recently concluded that oil giants such as BP—beloved of UK pension funds—could have their value cut in half if the world decides to tackle climate change. Coal companies can expect an even rougher ride, and yet our financial regulators still allow them to float on stock markets without mentioning in their share prospectuses that their assets may soon need to be written off.

But for now, the fuel is still flowing freely. And for as long as that continues, the global energy feedback loop will ensure that many of the things we assume will help may be ineffective—or even counterproductive. More efficient engines may simply enable more people to drive more cars over greater distances, triggering more road building, more trade and indeed more big suburban houses that take more energy to heat. New renewable or nuclear power sources might just lead to more economic activity, increasing demand and supply of all energy sources, including fossil fuels. And local carbon cuts caused by green choices, population decline or even new economic models may simply free up more fuel for use elsewhere.

Of course, oil, coal and gas use will level off eventually no matter what we do. Fossil fuels are a finite resource and each year they get more expensive relative to renewables and nuclear. But given the continued acceleration not just in fossil fuel extraction but in the production of cars, boilers, furnaces and power plants that need oil, coal and gas to function, there is zero prospect of that happening of its own accord any time soon. Forget peak oil caused by dwindling supplies. At least until we've cracked cheap carbon capture, we need to bring about peak fossil fuels. Voluntarily. And soon.

We know how to do it. A properly designed global cap and trade scheme is one option. Stiff taxes on the production or sale of carbon-based fuels is another. Or we could simply oblige companies taking carbon out of the ground to arrange for a rising share of what they extract to be buried again. Any of these models could bring down global emissions and stimulate an explosion of investment and innovation in clean and efficient energy systems. But there is no avoiding the unpalatable side-effects: spiralling fuel and energy prices; a write-off of fuel reserves worth many trillions of dollars; and a fierce global squabble about how to share out the fuels we do decide to burn.

How would all this affect the global economy, or pension funds, or the financial health of the Middle East, the US and other carbon-rich nations doing most to resist a global climate deal? For all the confident opinion on both sides, no one can say for sure, just as no one can be certain how human society will fare in a warming world. But with so much money and power bound up with oil, coal and gas, one thing seems clear: constraining global fossil fuel supplies will take bigger thinking, harder politics and—crucially—a whole lot more public pressure. Voluntary carbon cuts are a great start but they are no match for a system-level feedback in human energy use.

Globally, the vast majority of people want climate change dealt with. But can we bring ourselves to prioritise a safe planet over cheap fuels, flights, power and goods? Can we face calling on our leaders to end the double-think and constrain oil, coal and gas supplies on our behalf? Can humanity muster the restraint and cooperation needed to leave assets worth trillions in the ground?

The Power of Money and Advertising

Sandra Laville and David Pegg

Sandra Laville and David Pegg are both reporters at the Guardian.

Oil and gas companies are spending millions of dollars on campaigns to fight climate regulations at the same time as touting their dedication to a low-carbon future, according to a joint analysis by the *Guardian* and InfluenceMap.

Their global PR campaigns on social media promote a commitment to a green, low-carbon future, but across the US in particular, specific local campaigns are obstructing tighter regulations on fossil fuel extraction.

In many cases, oil and gas companies are using direct advertising but some targeted lobbying appears to be more opaque. It is channelled through so called "community" groups—which are being funded by fossil fuel companies.

A new study of Facebook's advertising disclosure platform by InfluenceMap suggests oil companies and their trade groups have spent $17m directly on political social media advertisements since May 2018.

ExxonMobil spent $9.6m—by far the biggest sum—ConocoPhillips $910,000 and BP $790,000.

These ads include PR highlighting low carbon alternatives and at the same time involve direct lobbying against climate initiatives and the promotion of continued fossil fuel extraction in the energy mix.

BP's "possibilities everywhere" ad campaign on Facebook was launched just weeks after it joined big oil companies to use a "community" group to fight against a bill restricting fracking in Colorado, known as Proposition 112.

"Fossil Fuel Firms' Social Media Fightback Against Climate Action," by Sandra Laville and David Pegg, with analytics from Michael Barton, Sam Cutler, and team, Guardian News and Media Limited, October 10, 2019. Reprinted by permission.

Prop 112 aimed to increase the distance fracking wells are set back from houses, schools and hospitals from 500ft (about 150 metres) to 2,500ft (760 metres).

It was designed to protect communities and the environment, and promote the transition from fossil fuels, according to those behind the bill.

But the campaign by a "grassroots" group Protect Colorado helped to defeat the bill by a margin of 200,000 votes last November. Protect Colorado's Facebook page and website list it as a community organisation.

They make no mention that the organisation was given $41 million by the oil and gas industry and its trade groups between January and December 2018, according to campaign declarations to the Colorado Secretary of State.

BP gave Protect Colorado $300,000 in October 2018, a month after relocating its US onshore headquarters from Houston to Denver. The move was to help it tap the state's estimated reserves of 1.3bn barrels of oil and exploit increased production, which has made Colorado the country's fifth largest oil producer.

Guardian analysis of Facebook's ad disclosure platform reveals Protect Colorado had an influence reach of up to 3.3 million impressions in the weeks before the vote, in a state with a population of about 5 million people.

The out-of-state fracking firms Noble Energy and Anadarko Petroleum Corporation, based in Houston, Texas, put $6m each into Protect Colorado.

The oil and gas firm ConocoPhillips gave the group $1m, Denver-based Liberty Oilfield Services provided $749,000 and the Colorado Petroleum Council gave $4.5m to Protect Colorado.

Anne Lee Foster, the communications director at Colorado Rising, which raised $1.2m for its campaign promoting Prop 112, said: "It felt like an attack on our democracy, where you have these corporations spending millions and millions of dollars, often out-of-state interests, fighting citizens who are simply trying to protect their families.

"We lost by 200,000 votes, so yes, 100% we believe the vote was swayed by the social media push they financed. They created doubt. They exploited people's fears that the setback would mean big job losses."

The *Guardian* contacted Protect Colorado but it failed to respond. The *Guardian* also contacted all the oil and gas companies involved in the campaigning.

BP confirmed it had opposed Prop 112. "BP is open to, and will continue to engage in, substantive discussions about regulatory efforts to address the impacts of oil and gas development.

"We also remain committed to safe and reliable operations in Colorado—and everywhere we operate—as we work to meet society's demand for cleaner, better energy."

At the time of going to press there were no other comments provided.

The use of groups that term themselves grassroots community organisations but are funded by major companies is known as "astroturfing."

In 2014, a leaked document from the Western States Petroleum Association—the oil and gas trade body in states including Washington, Oregon and California—detailed the use of such community groups to push back against climate campaigners and the anti-oil agenda—something WSPA described as "the worst of times."

Research for the *Guardian* by InfluenceMap has uncovered various examples of so called astro turfing. Within the Facebook adverts, the funders tend to be disclosed as the named group behind the adverts with no information on who ultimately controls these groups. Only through further research does oil company support become more clear.

In Texas a campaign opposing new regulations on oil pipelines in Senate bill 421 is led by Texans for Natural Gas, which is listed as a community group on Facebook.

It describes itself as a "grassroots organisation" that gives a voice to those who support Texas oil and natural gas production.

The Facebook ads against SB 421 are listed as being funded directly by Texans for Natural Gas. The small print at the bottom of the group's website states: "We are supported by five of the state's leading energy companies—Apache Corp, EnerVest, EOG Resources, Kinder Morgan and XTO Energy" (a subsidiary of ExxonMobil).

Measure G, a bill to ban new fracking and conventional oil and gas wells in the California county of San Luis Obispo, but allow existing facilities to continue, was defeated last year after an extensive industry-funded campaign against the proposed law, which spent more than $160,000 on more than 500 Facebook adverts, according to the ad library.

Major oil industry corporations donated about $8m to the No on Measure G campaign, according to local campaign finance filings. Chevron donated half that sum, while Aera Energy, a joint venture between Shell and ExxonMobil, contributed $900,000.

The campaign in support of the measure raised only $243,000 in the same period.

Shell said it opposed Measure G because "it would have shut down a century-old industry in the county, costing hundreds of local legacy jobs, millions in taxes to local coffers and cut off critical energy to an area of the country that has long struggled to keep up with growing demand.

"While we share the view that a low-carbon economy will only be possible through a combination of more renewables and biofuels, efficiency standards, CCS [carbon capture and storage] and a carbon tax, cleaner and more convenient hydrocarbons are still needed to provide a full suite of energy products for the growing global population—especially in areas of industry and transportation that are proving difficult to abate," a Shell spokesperson said.

Between September and November 2018, the No on Measure G campaign published several hundred Facebook adverts encouraging residents of San Luis Obispo to oppose the law, according to a *Guardian* analysis.

Most of the adverts suggested the measure would cause economic damage, such as job losses, or an increased reliance on foreign oil, and suggested continued fossil fuel use was part of a "transition to a clean energy economy."

Last year BP donated $13m to a campaign, also supported by Chevron, that successfully stopped a carbon tax in Washington state—$1m of which was spent on social media ads, research shows.

Going Green Requires Statutory Change

Mike Tidwell

Mike Tidwell is the founder and director of the Chesapeake Climate Action Network. He is also an author and a filmmaker.

The Copenhagen climate conference currently underway in Denmark has sparked global focus on "going green" in favor of environmentally friendly habits. But one environmental activist says that's a waste of time. Mike Tidwell, of the Chesapeake Climate Action Network, explains why he's skeptical of the green movement. Tidwell says the focus is a distraction from serious environmental action.

MICHAEL MARTIN, host: And now for another perspective on conscientious living. You try to be a good, green citizen, lowering the heat, biking to work, recycling your water bottles, better yet skipping the water bottles and going straight to the fountain. But what if it doesn't really matter? What if your individual efforts do very little to prevent global warming, except mostly making you feel a little bit better about yourself?

Mike Tidwell wrote an op-ed in this Sunday's *Washington Post* where he says stop going green, just stop it: no more compact fluorescent light bulbs, no more green wedding planning, no more organic toothpicks for holiday hors d'oeuvres. He goes on to say despite all our talk about washing clothes in cold water, we aren't making much of a difference. Mike Tidwell is executive director of the Chesapeake Climate Action Network, and he joins us now in our Washington, D.C., studio to talk more about this. Thanks for joining us.

Mr. MIKE TIDWELL (Executive Director, Chesapeake Climate Action Network): Thanks for having me.

"Environmentalist Says 'Going Green' Is a Waste of Time," by Mike Tidwell, National Public Radio Inc., December 8, 2009. Reprinted by permission.

MARTIN: That's kind of a shot across the bow there. How could it be bad to make individual efforts?

Mr. TIDWELL: It's not necessarily bad. I think everyone who truly understands the global climate crisis has a personal moral responsibility to do all they can in their personal life to have a lower impact. I certainly do. I drive a Prius, I'm a vegetarian, I have solar panels on my roof. I'm obnoxiously green. I'm hideously green.

MARTIN: Now you kind of cast a—the eye at me when I brought my paper script in instead of reading it off the screen. I saw it. Don't think I didn't see it. But anyway...

Mr. TIDWELL: The thing is, though, if that's our main emphasis is personal choice, then we lose. The problem is most people don't take voluntary action. Less than 10 percent of all our light bulbs, household light bulbs, are compact fluorescents. Only two and a half percent of auto sales are hybrid cars.

The problem is most people want statutory change. They want laws that lead to shared responsibility and shared benefits versus, well, if I go to all this trouble, and my neighbor doesn't, then I'm cleaning the air for him. I'm stopping global warming for him, too. That's not necessarily fair. I'd rather do it the way we've done it in the past.

For example, in the civil rights movement—which I talk about in the *Washington Post* op-ed—you know, we banned the practice of segregation. There comes a point when the moral, economic, social issue is so large that we have to make statutory changes. We did it for slavery, women's suffrage. Now we have to do it for climate change.

MARTIN: Well, you know, there's an argument that it has to be both/and, that one of the arguments about why we have seen the kind of ongoing resistance we have, in fact, seen to real integration, real integration, real social justice in this country, is that there was never that personal commitment on the part of key players—that you see it in the criminal justice system, for example, which remains biased, according to—if you just look at the data about how it affects different groups over others.

There are people who would argue that you can change their behavior, but you can't change people's hearts, and what some would say, if you don't change people's hearts, the behavior doesn't really change.

Mr. TIDWELL: Well, I'm old enough to have remembered the 1960s and went to school in some newly integrated public schools in the Deep South, and I know the world my parents grew up in in the Deep South and the world that I grew up in in the Deep South, and my experience was very different.

Here's the point: In the 1960s, we passed laws that banned, legally, discrimination in housing, employment, public accommodations. Now, did those laws instantaneously change every human heart in the American South and the rest of the nation? No, but we still made enormous progress, and all you have to do is look at who occupies the White House right now to know that it's a much different world.

Would Barack Obama even be president if we'd left civil rights to voluntary change, and let's do it one house at a time, one heart at a time? No. We banned certain practices, which have led to value changes.

MARTIN: Do you think, though, that there is enough of a consensus to demand the kinds of broad-based changes that you are saying are necessary? For example, you know, some parts of the world, there are very stringent measures in place, you know, high levels of taxation on energy consumption, for example, real investment in the most up-to-date technologies that are expected to be broadly applied.

We don't have that here, as you say, and I wonder if that is in part because you said at the beginning of our conversation that what people really want is kind of a broad-based, shared social investment so that they don't feel that they're making these efforts, and the other guys getting away with it.

The question I have is: Do people really want that? Do they really want that broad-based social investment? Because if that's the case, if they don't, then isn't that a matter of elites imposing their perspective on the country, and that isn't sustainable.

Mr. TIDWELL: We are being distracted by the go-green mania that results in very little change. Every time we pick up another green issue of *Vanity Fair*, every time we see "10 ways to go green at the office" on some Web site, we have the impression that broad change is happening when it's not.

Now, you look at nations that have, by statute, changed their societies in terms of energy, the Scandinavian nations, Japan, Europe, they use half the energy per capita as we do. They have laws that have penalized the actions they don't want, i.e. the burning of oil, coal and natural gas. They tax what they don't like, and they make free the things they do like.

In the United States, we don't do that. We make harmful fossil fuels almost free in comparison to the rest of the world. So we use a lot of it, we bake the planet, we create national insecurity in terms of buying oil from countries that don't like us.

Going green is great. I've done it. We need to do more. We can check that box. We've raised awareness. Now we have to change laws in this country that phase out rapidly the use of harmful fossil fuels.

MARTIN: Mike Tidwell is executive director of the Chesapeake Climate Action Network. He was kind enough to speak to us here in our Washington, D.C., studios. If you want to read the piece that we have been talking about, we'll have a link on our Web site. Just go to npr.org. Click on programs and then on TELL ME MORE. Mike Tidwell, thank you.

Mr. TIDWELL: Thank you.

Organizations to Contact

The editors have compiled the following list of organizations concerned with the issues debated in this book. The descriptions are derived from materials provided by the organizations. All have publications or information available for interested readers. This list was compiled on the date of publication of the present volume; the information provided here may change. Be aware that many organizations take several weeks or longer to respond to inquiries, so allow as much time as possible.

The American Petroleum Institute
200 Massachusetts Avenue NW
Suite 1100
Washington, DC 20001-5571
(202) 682-8000
website: www.api.org

The American Petroleum Institute is an organization representing the oil and gas industry in the United States. It advocates for safety in the industry and for policy that favors American oil and gas. The API conducts regular research, establishes industry standards, and hosts many trainings and seminars related to developments in oil and natural gas. The API publishes frequent press releases in addition to its studies and compiled statistics.

Brookings Institution
1775 Massachusetts Avenue NW
Washington, DC 20036
(202) 797-6000
email: communications@brookings.edu
website: www.brookings.edu

The Brookings Institution is a nonprofit public policy organization that conducts independent research. The Brookings Institution uses its research to provide recommendations that advance the goals of strengthening American democracy, fostering social welfare and security, and securing a cooperative international system. The organization publishes a variety of books, reports, and commentary that concern our approach to the economy.

Cato Institute
1000 Massachusetts Avenue NW
Washington, DC 20001-5403
(202) 842-0200
website: www.cato.org

The Cato Institute is a public policy research organization dedicated to the principles of individual liberty, limited government, free markets, and peace. The Cato Institute aims to provide clear, thoughtful, and independent analysis on vital public policy issues. The institute publishes numerous policy studies, two quarterly journals—*Regulation* and *Cato Journal*—and the bimonthly *Cato Policy Report*. It also has a wide array of articles, commentary, and Cato Studies regarding the green and brown economies.

The Green Economy Coalition
International Institute of Environment & Development
80-86 Grays Inn Road
London WC1X 8NH
United Kingdom
website: www.greeneconomycoalition.org

The Green Economy Coalition is an organization concerned with fighting climate change by advocating for green economy transitions. The group consists of over 50 NGOs, businesses, and organizations and is funded in part by the European Union. The organization works to connect these groups and influence decisions related to environmental policy. It publishes regular articles, case studies, and press releases related to green energy, the green economy, and climate change.

**The International Association of Oil and
Gas Producers**
1577 Memorial Drive
Suite 250
Houston, TX 77079
(713) 261-0411
email: reception@iogp.org
website: www.iogp.org

The IOGP is a group of businesses that produce and sell oil around the world. The organization serves to protect those interests and share best practices in safety, environmental and social responsibility, and operations. The IOGP also runs several external initiatives to improve standards and practices in the oil industry. It publishes a regular *Pulse* newsletter as well as press releases, position statements, and policy and data updates.

**The Organization for Economic Co-operation and
Development (OECD)**
OECD Washington Center
1776 I Street NW
Suite 450
Washington, DC 20006
(202) 785-6323
email: washington.contact@oecd.org
website: https://www.oecd.org/unitedstates/

The Organization for Economic Co-operation and Development is an international group that seeks to enhance trade relations and economic development between partner members. Member countries are limited to democracies with a market economy. Its current goals include shaping policies that promote economic growth, while considering equality and the environment.

The Organization of Petroleum Exporting Countries
Helferstorferstrasse 17, A-1010
Vienna, Austria
website: www.opec.org/opec_web/en/index.htm

OPEC is an international organization consisting of 13 member nations that collaborate around the issue of petroleum-based policy. It seeks stabilization of the oil market and economic and political conditions that favor oil exporting nations. OPEC publishes a monthly *Oil Market Report* and *Oil Bulletin*, in addition to its *Annual Statistical Bulletin*. The reports indicate trends in production output, exporting and importing, the refining process, and more.

The United Nations Environment Programme
United Nations Avenue, Gigiri
PO Box 30552, 00100
Nairobi, Kenya
email: unep-newsdesk@un.org
website: https://www.unenvironment.org

The United Nations Environment Programme is a branch of the UN that deals with environmental policy and that assists nations in meeting their sustainable development goals. Deeply concerned with climate change, the Environment Programme seeks to provide resources and leadership in green policy so as to improve quality of life around the world. The UN Environment Programme publishes an annual report, emissions gap reports, and numerous other studies and findings throughout the year.

The World Bank
1818 H Street NW
Washington, DC 20433 USA
(202) 473-1000
website: https://www.worldbank.org

The World Bank serves as an international financial organization with the goal of reducing poverty around the world. The bank provides loans and grants to countries seeking aid for development projects and it aims to make those results measurable and effective through policy advice and knowledge sharing. It has a regular newsletter as well as numerous op-eds, press releases, and formal studies. Many of these address the debate over investment in a green economy.

The World Resources Institute
10 G Street NE
Suite 800
Washington, DC 20002
(202) 729-7600
website: www.wri.org

The World Resources Institute is an international research organization focused on making change at the intersection of the environment and development. The WRI conducts original research investigating sustainable strategies, then works together with communities and governments to implement successful tactics. The WRI publishes a weekly *WRI Digest* in addition to its research projects and the hard data utilized in those studies.

Bibliography

Books

Ricardo Abramovay. *Beyond the Green Economy*. New York, NY: Routledge, 2016.

Edward Barbier, et al. *A New Blueprint for a Green Economy*. New York, NY: Routledge, 2013.

S. W. Carmalt. *The Economics of Oil: A Primer Including Geology, Energy, Economics, Politics*. New York, NY: Springer International Publishing, 2017.

Molly Scott Cato. *Green Economics: An Introduction to Theory, Policy and Practice*. New York, NY: Routledge, 2012.

Gareth Dale and Manu V. Mathai. *Green Growth: Ideology, Political Economy and the Alternatives*. Delhi, India: Aakar Books, 2017.

David C. Fessler. *The Energy Disruption Triangle: Three Sectors That Will Change How We Generate, Use, and Store Energy*. Hoboken, NJ: Wiley, 2019.

Andrew Heintzman. *The New Entrepreneurs: Building a Green Economy for the Future*. Toronto, ON: House of Anansi Press, 2011.

Xiaoyi Mu. *The Economics of Oil and Gas*. Newcastle upon Tyne, UK: Agenda Publishing, 2020.

Adrian C. Newton and Elena Cantarello. *An Introduction to the Green Economy: Science, Systems and Sustainability*. New York, NY: Routledge, 2014.

Robert Pollin. *Greening the Global Economy*. Cambridge, MA: The MIT Press, 2015.

Slawomir Raszewski. *The International Political Economy of Oil and Gas*. New York, NY: Palgrave Macmillan, 2018.

Robert B. Richardson. *Building a Green Economy: Perspectives from Ecological Economics.* East Lansing, MI: Michigan State University Press, 2013.

Helen Thompson. *Oil and the Western Economic Crisis.* New York, NY: Palgrave Macmillan, 2018.

Barbara Unmüßig, Lili Fuhr, and Thomas Fatheuer. *Inside the Green Economy: Promises and Pitfalls.* Cambridge, UK: UIT Cambridge Ltd., 2016.

Daniel Yergin. *The New Map: Energy, Climate, and the Clash of Nations.* New York, NY: Penguin Press, 2020.

Periodicals and Internet Sources

Edward Barbier, "The Green Economy Post Rio+20," *Science*, November 16, 2012. https://science.sciencemag.org/content/338/6109/887.summary?casa_token=3mQfiS4txnI AAAAA:2XmDWBntbLR5KNrdjXTrrwtzqnPhO2MQlK_7 auxpOEVncJ7T4tTlLZl-F6QvRPeUTxzdBbZNtkFfjw.

Olivia Bina, "The Green Economy and Sustainable Development: An Uneasy Balance?" *Environment and Planning C: Government and Policy*, vol. 31, no. 6, 2013.

Heidi Garrett-Peltier, "Green Versus Brown: Comparing the Employment Impacts of Energy Efficiency, Renewable Energy, and Fossil Fuels Using an Input-Output Model," *Economic Modelling*, vol. 61, 2017.

Sri Mulyani Indrawati, "Why Green Development Is So Important," World Economic Forum. www.weforum.org/agenda/2015/07/why-green-development-is-so-important/.

Gopal Kadekodi, "Is a 'Green Economy' Possible?" *Economic and Political Weekly*, June 22, 2013.

National Association of Counties, "Growing a Green Local Economy: County Strategies for Economic, Workforce and Environmental Innovation," Green Government Initiative,

May 2010. https://www.naco.org/sites/default/files /documents/Counties_Growing_Green_Local_Economy_-_ June_2010.pdf.

Ethan Pollack, "Counting up to Green: Assessing the Green Economy and Its Implications for Growth and Equity," Economic Policy Institute, October 10, 2012. https://www .epi.org/publication/bp349-assessing-the-green-economy/.

Stanley Reed, "With Much of the World's Economy Slowed Down, Green Energy Powers On," *New York Times*, June 30, 2020. www.nytimes.com/2020/06/30/business/renewable -energy.html.

Clive L. Spash, "Editorial: Green Economy, Red Herring," *Environmental Values*, vol. 21, no. 2, 2012.

Paul Stevens, "The Role of Oil and Gas in the Economic Development of the Global Economy," Oxford Scholarship Online, Oxford University Press. universitypressscholarship .com/view/10.1093/oso/9780198817369.001.0001 /oso-9780198817369-chapter-4.

UN Environment, "Green Economy," UNEP - UN Environment Programme. www.unenvironment.org/regions/asia-and -pacific/regional-initiatives/supporting-resource-efficiency /green-economy.

Index

5